THE DANCE OF EGO AND ESSENCE

CONFESSIONS OF A DIVINE DIVA

Dr. Pamela Gerali

The Dance of Ego and Essence
Confessions of a Divine Diva
by Dr. Pamela Gerali

Published by Mason Works Press, Boulder, Colorado.

For information, please contact Kathy Mason, Publisher,
at kathy@masonworksmarketing.com,
or write to Mason Works Press,
6525 Gunpark Dr. #370-426,
Boulder, CO 80301.

Cover and Interior Design by Kathy Mason and Maryann Sperry
Cover photo by Jim Gerali
Dancer Illustration by R. Anne Remington

ISBN-13: 978-0-9983209-6-0

First Edition
Library of Congress Control Number: 2021919416
Published in the United States of America
Printed in the United States of America

TESTIMONIALS

"As a recovering academic, researcher, creator of 'transformational' frameworks, and catalyst of paradigm change, I have sought to explain the evolutionary path of spiritual awakening in words, concepts, diagrams, and models for two decades. Happily, the universe has dissuaded me from continuing this 'futile' undertaking several times.

Then I read this quite astonishing book, and it does just that – and from multiple angles to boot. Dr. Gerali is indeed the ***Divine Diva seeker*** in the book's title whose apparent **Confessions –** I prefer to call them 'roadmaps to deeper conscious living' – are the significant insights, revelations and inner transformations she experienced from her forty-day retreat into the darkness and deceits of her less-than-conscious life, and what it took to transcend them.

Her gifts as a teacher of deep understanding come through in the story telling that reveals the catalyst for each of forty significant shifts of consciousness and the revelations that accompany each. The forty are sure to get the attention of anyone committed to spiritual growth; each being a clear reminder of the states of mind and life situations that erode the joy of being fully 'awake'. I observed them to be forty completely familiar aspects of life that serve as roadblocks or barriers to the 'bliss' that she earnestly sought to experience, and that fully conscious living ultimately offers. One by one she examines them, describes how they affected her life, and portrays the shift to its complementary state of higher manifestation.

My admiration for the book took another leap upward in the book's relatively short concluding section. Here I discovered the beautifully constructed wisdom in her *Blueprint for the Human Spirit.* Its frameworks, mapping of historical and cultural archetypes, and five dimensions and multiple stages of living summarized volumes of deeply considered knowledge in a few diagrams that immediately earned my deep admiration. Each diagram deserves major attention, repeated reflection, and further elaboration – hopefully in Dr. Gerali's next book. I can't wait."

> **Dr. William Spady**, Leadership and Transformational Outcome-Based Education Expert, author of ***Outcome-Based Education's Empowering Essence***

"Dr. Pamela Gerali's ***Dance of Ego and Essence*** is an inspiring and extraordinary journaling experience! It's an absolute must for anyone on a spiritual path with a desire to delve deeply into their healing process and gain greater self-awareness."

Andi Goldman, M.A., Holistic Psychotherapist and co-author of ***The Humming Effect***

"In ***Dance of Ego and Essence,*** Dr. Pamela Gerali splendidly inspires us in her heartening and hopeful new book on how to live in our higher Essence. Her warm and engaging personal stories lift us up, and her honesty about her own life hurdles and flaws gives us comfort in accepting our own. The 40 daily ways to heal our attitudes lead us into discovering how to have a peaceful heart, and the affirmations show us how to let go of what has held us back. I highly recommend this beautiful book to anyone seeking self-acceptance."

Charol Messenger, author of ***Your Awakening Attitude of Service,*** and honoree of Marquis Who's Who in America 2020

"Dr. Gerali takes us on a journey of self-discovery and shows us the power of inquiry using her Blueprint for the Human Spirit along with insightful personal stories. Reading this book will help you shed light on beliefs, behaviors, and thoughts that don't support you. It uncovers the quiet saboteurs that we do not see without this deep dive method of questioning ourselves and replacing our old belief with an empowering affirmation. If you are looking for deep personal transformation, this book is for you."

Vickie Helm, CEO and bestselling author of ***The She Myth Redefining Women In Business***

"One of the biggest challenges we all face, yet most often avoid to fully meet, is how to embrace and navigate the dualities and contradictions within our own self, and the world at large. This avoidance is, in my observations, a root cause in our suffering that blocks our inner evolution. Until we can embrace and bring compassion and healing to our 'shadow' aspects we remain deeply fragmented and out of reach to living a fulfilling and embodied life as a whole person, which is what we all long for. There is hidden wisdom within our shadows to be gleaned that can deepen our insight and understanding of our dual nature, call it our high self and lower natured self, that can free us in so many ways. Pamela's offering here is an invitation that opens the door to meet our other half, so to speak, with curiosity, love and kindness. This is a path that leads to freedom and empowerment. Pamela candidly shares her journey down this path which will surely encourage the reader to explore, forgive and uncover their inner treasures and wisdoms that await to be encountered with love. I highly recommend this book to all looking to live a fully authentic, joy filled life."

Luannah Arana, Owner and Operator of Serenity by the Sea Retreats and Wellness and Best-Selling Author of ***Resilience, Grace and the Art of Showing Up***

"Dr. Pamela Gerali has quilted together jewels of experiences, sifted through "whacks" from the Universe and written an engaging, insightful spiritual odyssey. It is truly a page-turner and after your first read, you may want to read it again over a 40-day period as it was written. Each day, Pamela stripped another layer as she dove deep into life's trials and triumphs until reaching spiritual nudity and a place of peace, wonder and continuous evolution. She invites the reader to take her 40-day challenge and reap similar benefits while learning to dance with your inner divine. Take the Joy-Ride!"

Dr. Noel K. Marshall, CoFounder: www.LightPartners.org, CoFounder: www.cocreatorsconvergence.com

"To be Fearless and Free, you have to uncover the programs that are running your life. It's a messy process- but so worth the effort! The ***Dance of Ego and Essence*** will guide you through a 40-day process to discover your path to liberation."

Victoria Reynolds, Best-Selling Author of ***Transcending Fear, The Journey to Freedom and Fulfillment***

"The predominant obstacle blocking most women from living from their "Possibility Space" and creatively problem-solving is their perspectives of their reality. Dr. Pamela Gerali courageously evaluates 40 different perspectives in her new book, ***Dance of Ego and Essence- Confessions of a Divine Diva.*** I benefited from her "dance" and I know that you will too!"

Elsie Ritzenhein, Best Selling author of ***Awakening Your Creative Voice: Women in a World of Possibility***

"In this powerful new book, Dr. Pamela Gerali draws the curtain to courageously reveal her inner conversations with her shadow self. In a series of 40 daily confessions, she invites us to face what we keep hidden, and rise like her to a state of Essence."

Maryse Cardin, author of ***Self Talk Love for Sensitives: Ease Anxiety and Awaken to the Gifts of Being a Highly Sensitive Woman.***

Dedication

To all who are committed to raising their awareness and expressing their divinity through their humanity

Acknowledgments

A special thank you to all who have made this book and my work possible, including:

Jim, my loving and supportive husband—for your gift of photography, assistance with editing, and for your endless love and encouragement

Roberta, my soul sister—for years of support and for editing the second edition of this book

My Family—from whom I have learned the most and will continue to learn

Marcy, my dear friend—for editing my original journal and supporting my efforts

Kathy, my kindred spirit and consultant—for assisting in my efforts to share the *Blueprint* with the world

Anne, my friend and colleague—for years of support and for creating the dancer illustrations

My spiritual mothers, sisters, and dedicated teachers—for your love, encouragement, support, and input

Table of Contents

Foreword

What does it mean to walk the path of true healing? To travel to the depths of our reality, beyond hope, beyond fear to uncover, examine, and free ourselves from the roots of our modern feminine malaise?

The Dance of Ego and Essence and the Blueprint for the Human Spirit Dr. Pamela Gerali has brought forth and fully articulated is very much in keeping with seekers throughout the ages. It appeals to those who have journeyed inward to listen to the essential voice of spirit and unravel the mystery of who they really are. This is not an easy path. We have been conditioned through the chaos and confusion of our current era in history and the cycle of the Ages to be disconnected from our essential nature. We have been separated from the awakened God/Goddess within and from the divine essence revealed in all of the world's great spiritual traditions.

From birth, unless we are born into a rare family with the ability to recognize our innate gifts, we are indoctrinated. Our perceptions, attitudes, beliefs, responses, mannerisms, and expressions are conditioned by familial patterns, religious and societal agendas, motives that often lead us to self-judgment, addictions, egotism, competition, jealousy, greed, and so much more. Metaphorically, this behavioral patterning is often expressed as veils or layers of an onion that obscure our true nature. So how do we lift the veil? How do we unpeel the layers to get to the heart, the diamond essence of who we truly are?

In this book, Pamela fearlessly examines the diverse aspects of her life experience in a very honest and open way which is enlivening, inspiring, and uplifting for us all. She had the courage, and the commitment to really observe herself, open her heart and mind to us, revealing a path by which we too can begin to discern the small egoic self from the immensity and life-affirming power of our own essential spirit.

As a dancer from the time of gestation in my mother's womb, through my childhood, for my entire life, in cultures and traditions throughout the world, I have felt the power of life's dance, the enlivening current of Shakti, Qi, and Prana, the life-force flowing through my body. So, for me, it is fascinating that Pamela uses the metaphor of the dance, of Lila, the divine play of life, to describe her personal healing and transformative experiences.

Dance music story. These are time-honored ways for us to connect, heal, discover, and experience true community. For centuries, women would gather together and tell their stories to assist each other through life's passages. The women of this Sacred Sisterhood were there for each other through times of joy and pain, through birth and death, through illness and times in which it seemed there was no way out. But somehow, during this modern age, these essential feminine ways have been repressed and distorted. Instead of this loving sense of communion, competition, jealousy, anger, and deception took root.

For many years, I have been immersed in discovering the myths, stories, teachings, and practices of the Divine Feminine in cultures around the world. My dancing feet and passionate spirit were set on this path through the blessing of my Guruji Sitara Devi, Queen of Kathak dance of North India, and early Bollywood star. While living with her in Mumbai in the traditional guru-disciple manner, I had the honor of having these ancient, feminine teachings directly transmitted to me. I was able to fully perceive, experience, and embody the qualities and manifestations of the Goddess in all her beauty, power, sensuality, love, and compassion.

This powerful transmission pours through me and throughout the ensuing years has been expressed through the mediums of dance, writing, film, music, and more. As part of a living lineage handed down for centuries, my calling, like Pamela's, is to assist women in creating a new paradigm in which these ancient values of truth, virtue, integrity, compassion, and communion are brought forth into this time. We work in emergence; we listen to each other; we feel each other. We open our senses to experience the beauty of Mother Nature. We dance together. We play together, and out of that joy, that intimacy, we dream a new world into being.

I feel that this book holds the keys to that dream of personal and collective freedom, self-discovery, and healing on many levels. It is a contemporary expression of the guidance inherent in the circles of the ancient Sacred Sisterhood that helps us grow and discover the true essence of our being. This has always been pure, clear, and flawless.

As the chapters unfold, Pamela fearlessly strips away all that is superfluous--the confusion, pain, and needless suffering in herself. She releases conditioned attitudes and transforms fearful happenings until she comes to the sacred heart of her experience, the understanding of who she really is. Pamela teaches us about the power of silence and listening to one's inner voice. She speaks about the sense of presence, true presence, and awareness. And through this inward journey, this lifting of the veils, she reveals the artifice and contrivances of ego and the fundamental radiance of essence.

Now at this time in the world, ego can be useful. But ego needs to be in balance with essence. This blueprint that she received and brings to us all is more than a journey of self-revelation and instruction. It is also a work of art. Pouring out of Pamela's experiences is a blueprint for the human spirit.

She teaches us to dance with our emotions, riding the waves of our life force energy, our mood swings. She teaches us about the relationship between our thoughts, emotions, and physical manifestation, and our pain and suffering, stripping away all that is superfluous to uncover our true essential nature. Beyond ego, beyond resistance.

At the end of each chapter, based upon her own insights and deep personal exploration, she offers inspirational affirmations to help each and every one of us to persevere, to trust. She explores disciplines such as working with diet and food. She uses the power of listening to our own bodies to find balance, discovering our inner guru, and trusting our own intuitive knowing. She teaches us how to rest, let go, free our minds, relax, release, and renew.

Like Inanna, from the Sumerian mythology, she descends. She also takes the path of descent into the darkness of ego, peeling away her judgments, expectations, impatience, anxiety, and attachments. She brings her own experience into all of these feminine issues and more, helping us work with our sensitivity to criticism, how to get out of the way and allow the divine spirit to flow through us, to embrace life.

Through the heartfelt expression of her journey, she teaches us to ask for help and let go of control, freeing ourselves from guilt and unworthiness, let go of emotional scars, negativity, and that feminine desire to fully please others beyond everything else. In doing so, she brings forth her understanding of the true nature of love and the bliss of realizing our highest potential.

Through the medium of her personal experiences, Pamela explores how we can remain focused and not get distracted by the pressures of daily life. This is especially critical during these shadowy times in which we are constantly surrounded by fear-based programming, divisiveness, and the repression of our true open spacious nature. And she reveals how the weeding out of all of this programming, all of these conditioned attitudes and perceptions, we can begin to experience a joy, bliss, and freedom that is rare.

In gratitude and appreciation for this mythic quest and revelation of the spirit,

Sharron Rose, President, Sacred Mysteries Productions

Author of *The Path of the Priestess: A Guidebook for Awakening the Divine Feminine*

Producer/Composer, *The Nectar of Bliss: Embracing the Divine Feminine Spirit*

Foreword

"Womenkind, rise up and take hold of your true feminine power. Dare to lift the veils that have obscured your mind and begin to see from deep within your heart. Have the courage to swim against the rising tide of darkness that constantly threatens to overcome you. Do not be afraid to risk all, do not be afraid to live in truth. Look into the eyes of your children, into the eyes of your mates, parents, sisters, and brothers. See the shining light of spirit trapped within them, imprisoned by the vicissitudes of this dark age. Understand that your loved ones are just as confused and afraid as you are. They are waiting for their mothers, teachers, healers, and wise women to wake up from their long painful sleep and once again, guide them toward true liberation."

From The Path of the Priestess

Introduction, Intention & Invitation

The Universe provides many opportunities for growth. Some life lessons emerge as physical crises, fiscal challenges, damaged relationships, or lost career opportunities. Regardless of what obstacle we encounter, we will always evolve, unless we wallow in self-pity or refuse to see the blessing in the misfortune. We will learn if we are open, ready, and willing.

My latest opportunity for soul growth came in the form of a health issue. I had viral thyroiditis and was flatlined for six months. For a caregiver who is typically filled with vitality, this was a low blow. It tested my patience and challenged my commitments to live purposefully.

After I recovered, I was ready to refocus on my life's work. For nearly two years, I had not written about the *Blueprint for the Human Spirit®* (See My Divine Choreographer below) nor shared its sacred wisdom. Also, I had not performed any intuitive healings. With my energy restored, I was ready to begin anew, but I had no idea where to begin.

Before going to bed I typed an affirmation into my iPhone: *"I am open, ready, and willing to focus on my work with the Blueprint and gratefully receive inspiration on what project to work on first. And so it is."*

I had no idea where spirit would lead, however, I assumed I would be guided to complete one of the many abandoned projects in my files. But NO! I awoke knowing that I was supposed to rise early, meditate, bare my soul, and journal confessions for forty days.

Forty—The Number of Rebirth

Imagine my chagrin at the thought of spilling my guts for forty days. I am far from perfect but was surprised that I had so much to confess. After all, I am a spiritual teacher and intuitive healer! I had released a lot of baggage and old beliefs over the past twenty years. Forty days also seemed a little ambitious since I had not dedicated my efforts to a project for quite some time. Regardless, I was ready, and since I had asked what to do, I heeded the guidance.

A little research revealed interesting spiritual symbolism. Forty is the number of rebirth and purification. Many sacred texts in addition to the Bible include stories with this number. I am aware of the forty-day flood, the forty years the Israelites waited to reach the Promised Land, and forty days Jesus spent in the wilderness. I also know that human gestation is forty weeks. Obviously, the number forty holds great significance for spiritual growth and transformation.

I began my forty-day experience a few days later. I set my alarm for 6:00 AM and prepared to rise early. I was not clear on what I should do but vowed to go to my sacred space and open my heart and mind. I began by lighting a candle, taking a few deep breaths, and sitting in the silence. I waited a few minutes, and a word came to mind. A visceral reaction in the form of a confession quickly emerged. Relevant stories and experiences popped into my awareness. After a few minutes, I picked up my journal and began to write.

From Ego to Essence

Words flowed onto the page. I easily and effortlessly wrote for an hour without censoring what emerged. I was amazed that my hyperactive body and fidgety, judgmental mind did not interfere. I was also surprised when the journal entry ended with a summary of what I had learned and an affirmation. This positive statement about my new beliefs and behaviors was the opposite of the opening confession. One day at a time for forty days, I clearly recalled how the tango of Ego and Essence unfolded and how I had made a quantum leap in awareness.

To say this exercise was transforming is putting it mildly. Every day I received a word and I confessed things I had forgotten or stuffed so far down that I had to dig deep into the painful past to uncover. With each revelation, I was liberated, and I let go of more pain, guilt, and fear. I owned up to so many shortcomings and mistakes, I feared no one would respect me or believe I could guide them. I released so much that Essence, the Divine Diva, emerged in all her glory after years of pretending. The façade of piety was discarded along with past attempts to reconcile faults and faux pas. All that remained was the truth. I was exposed, stripped spiritually naked. This purification process restored innocence that had long been forgotten. Old beliefs that continued to haunt me were brought to light and were replaced with authenticity.

Before this life-changing experience, I had not embraced the idea of confession. My childhood was shadowed with fundamentalism and extreme guilt that I escaped when I went to college. Trips to the altar, begging and crying for forgiveness, had not brought relief. I rejected this practice along with the conservative religion. I also bought into Ego's trap of hiding transgressions and weaknesses behind education, good works, and cleverness. Now everything was brought out in the open for me to face head on and expose to the world.

By sharing my forty-day experience, I have come clean. I have removed layers of protection that hid what I did not want anyone to know about me. Transparency is not an easy dance. When you air dirty laundry, you must be ready for a little fallout. I have no idea what will transpire, but I trust you will be inspired to follow my lead. Perhaps like me, you will learn that you are both fully human and fully divine, doing your best every moment while still making blunders. Regardless, I am revealing my experience as another way to share my gifts with seekers around the world.

The Symbolism of Dance

Dancing was forbidden in the ultraconservative Christian church and home where I was raised. It was just one activity on an exhaustive list of "thou shalt nots" that included watching TV, shopping on Sundays, wearing makeup, slacks, and shoes without toes and heels, cutting our hair, listening to rock or pop music, drinking alcohol, dancing… We were punished and threatened with hell fire for these "sins" and many other infractions.

I could never understand why dancing was taboo. Like the teens in the movie *Footloose*, I looked up Bible verses and read how dance was a form of praise and worship. And like most teens, I disobeyed my parents. My older sister and I spent many evenings dancing to forty-five records at our cousin's home. Although shy and insecure, I loved to dance. I loved the freedom to move and express myself in the safe confines of her bedroom. Since I was hyperactive, dancing also was a way for me to release pent-up energy.

Some people dance because it is a way of life, a calling, passion, or chosen profession. They crave the ecstasy of performing and thrive on accolades from audiences. Dancing may be their livelihood, and how they support themselves and their families. However, the majority of humankind dance for fun, to get in shape, celebrate, meet a mate, or socialize. Regardless of our motivation, dancing offers many benefits and is a perfect symbol for holistic transformation.

Dancing promotes health and wellness by enhancing mobility, flexibility, endurance, and cardiovascular fitness. It increases oxygen to the brain, boosting mental function. Dancing provides a meditative moment where we let go of thoughts and are fully emersed in the present. We escape the mundane and release negative emotions. While dancing with others, we experience oneness and intimacy, and we reinforce deep bonds that unite us with our partners.

From a spiritual perspective, dancing is a form of prayer and praise. While experiencing the ecstasy of dance, we commune with God and all Creation.

Through motions, positions, and expressions, we convey our devotion to and sense divine union with a Higher Power and all that is. Through dance, we also reveal our sacred self and know wholeness within. Our inner diva expresses her divinity with each sacred step.

Dancing symbolically demonstrates how we learn from each other. I once performed an intuitive healing for a friend whose husband suffered a paralyzing stroke. He had aphasia and could not communicate. During the session, however, he shared a message through me. It included imagery of his favorite pastime, dancing.

> *"I reach out and hold you close and sway with the music. I know that we are moving in this awesome, divine rhythm of life, smooth and flowing. The dance of life. I have danced with abandon through our relationships. I have danced the dance of husband, lover, father, employee, and friend. I give sincere thanks for every partner that I have danced with. You have enriched my life. From you I have learned and grown, and I have become the man that you have known all these years. You have taught me how to love. You have taught me how to live, how to be the true spirit that I am. If you knew, if you only knew how much I adore each and every one of you, you would know only a tiny, tiny bit of how your love has enriched my life."*

As human beings, we dance in two worlds—earthly and eternal. Depending on what is happening in our lives, we may lean more toward one or the other. Usually in times of crisis, we revert to old egoic patterns. When in the flow, we dance in harmony with our true essential nature.

This exercise has taught me that we need not dance as one or the other. Instead, it revealed the importance of merging Ego with Essence. Instead of eliminating Ego, we honor it and use our humanness to fully engage with others. Our uniqueness, personality, and inner qualities reflect our divine nature. We express our divinity through our humanity.

Each partner in the dance of life teaches us something special. Each step leads us toward greater awareness and unity. When we reach the desired state of oneness, our divine diva emerges in all her radiance, opens her arms, and embraces everyone in a sacred dance.

Your Rebirthing Dance

The greatest thing we can do to uplift humanity is to raise our own awareness. I am committed to this on a personal level. I also hope that you will consider joining me in a forty-day journaling and meditation experience to cleanse your soul. It will transform your life.

If you are reading this spiritual book, I can only assume that you are open, ready, and willing to move forward on your path toward greater awareness. While reading this book, no doubt you will also come face to face with your own issues. In fact, it can be very revealing and may help you release old limiting beliefs and behaviors.

Through radical honesty, it is possible to heal wounds, release fears, and transform traumas that prevent us from fully embracing and expressing the truth of our being. So instead of just reading about my experience, I encourage you to take this process and information to heart. Instead of just being entertained, engage in your own forty-day transforming experience. You can also be reborn and restore innocence with a commitment to honesty and transparency.

Although painful memories may rise to the surface as you read this book, know that you will also experience extreme joy. Shortly after beginning this process, I was so light and free that I felt as if I was flying. I was dancing on air. I know that you, too, will experience extreme freedom as you resolve issues from your past. You will be filled with elation as you begin to dance in harmony with Essence.

With each day's topic and reading, search your soul and write your own confessions. Sit in the silence and allow your memories about the topic to flow to the surface. Record what you have learned and write your own affirmations so you can more fully integrate the information presented into a life-changing experience.

As you examine your life and eliminate old, limiting beliefs, you can be freed from the "unholy trinity" of guilt, shame, and fear, free to be all that you are meant to be. You will feel empowered to live more authentically and purposefully, realizing your fullest potential as an ambassador of love. When you open to higher guidance and change your perceptions, you can make that leap of faith across the chasm to merge Ego and Essence.

To benefit the most from this experience, consider following the steps below:

- Pause in the silence and in the Presence; affirm that you have an open heart, mind, and spirit.
- Read the daily passage from The Dance of Ego and Essence: Confessions of a Divine Diva below.
- Allow your memories and feelings about the topic of the day to rise to the surface.
- Pick up your pen, write your own confession, and share your experiences, thoughts, and emotions.
- Ask for higher guidance on the topic and write what comes to you.
- Write your own Affirmation, indicating what you intend to "be" in the future. "I am…"
- Make a commitment to "walk your talk."
- Express gratitude for greater awareness and for the healing experience.
- Enjoy the freedom and elation this exercise brings by making a commitment to be authentic, bringing your thoughts, feelings, and actions into alignment with what you know to be true.

Study Group Option

On my spiritual journey I have found sacred circles to be of great benefit. Invite other kindred spirits to join you on this holy dance into the depths of your being. The benefits of a sacred study group are many.

- "Change partners" will help you remain true to your commitment.
- Their support will uplift and empower you as you release pain from the past.
- You can laugh, cry, and celebrate together as you move forward on your inner journey.
- Others can help hold you accountable as you commit to changing beliefs, adopting new behaviors, and dealing with a painful past. Together you can affirm and realize greater alignment with your authentic self.

The options for organizing your circle are many. Use consensus to determine logistics on how to proceed, including when, where, how long, and how frequently to meet.

May you be richly blessed on your dance of self-discovery, embracing and expressing Essence as the divine diva that you are.

Pamela

Prologue: My Divine Choreographer

Before I share my 40-day transforming dance of ego and essence, I would like to introduce my divine choreographer, the *Blueprint for the Human Spirit®*. This inner teacher appeared quite unexpectedly and guided my spiritual awakening. It emerged like magic into a sacred matrix and provided answers to my many questions about life. It is a road map or instruction manual for the human experience.

An Unlikely Recipient

To say that I am an unlikely recipient of this transforming dance is putting it mildly. I was raised in an ultra-conservative home in a small town in Northwestern Pennsylvania. The fundamental church we attended had an exhaustive list of "thou shalt nots" that were enforced with threats of severe punishment and hellfire. My childhood was filled with the "unholy trinity" of guilt, shame, and fear. I was a victim of religious abuse.

When I went to college, I left the legalistic, negative teachings behind and focused on nursing and public health. My scientific training encouraged me to be goal-oriented, analytical, rational, and skeptical. Although I was extremely successful from a career perspective, I was emotionally shut down. My life was also devoid of anything spiritual. I didn't know difference between religion and spirituality.

For twenty years, I was a perfectionistic workaholic. I dedicated my life to helping others and saving lives as a program director for non-profit health organizations. Then the Universe intervened. My employer sent me to an intensive leadership program at the Center for Creative Leadership in Greensboro, North Carolina.

This was my first experience with visioning and journaling. Eight hours of questionnaires, including some completed by colleagues, subordinates, and superiors, provided great insight. This was the first time I looked inside, and I didn't like everything I discovered. So, I decided to dance a new dance.

A Novice Dancer

Since my job was no longer compatible with my new vision, I retired early and became a spiritual junkie. I read every spiritual book I could get my hands on, attended every holistic workshop within driving distance, and tried every practice recommended by mystics and masters both past and present. Nothing seemed to work for me, but I continued my exhaustive search. I was also extremely fearful of being led down a wrong path. I didn't trust myself to know if I was on target or if I had become a victim of another religious charlatan.

In July 1995, a medical intuitive revealed I would work with shapes and share what I learned with the world. Two days later, I began receiving divine downloads. I was awakened at 3:30 a.m. and laid in bed in a state of open awareness. For over an hour information flowed into my awareness. I retained as much as I could, then got up and entered what I learned into my computer.

These transmissions occurred three or four mornings a week for six months. One concept at a time, the *Blueprint for the Human Spirit* evolved in harmony with my unfolding. No doubt my rational mind processed the information and helped it meld into a beautiful, understandable format. See the simplified *Blueprint* Matrix below.

This holistic matrix also emerged with complementary shapes and energy. It grew from a simple Mind-Body-Spirit triangle into an elegant design with five dimensions—physical, mental, emotional, intuitive, and spiritual, and five fields of existence—quantum, self, social, global, and eternal.

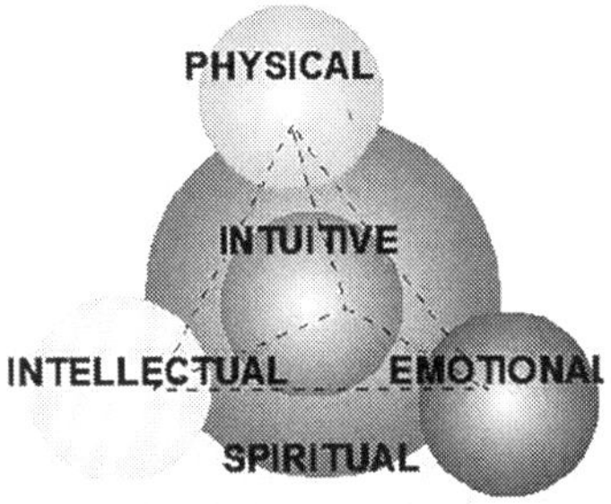

DIMENSIONS of LIFE

At that time, I was not aware of sacred geometry. I did not understand much of what had been transmitted, but the *Blueprint* continued to develop and guide my spiritual awakening.

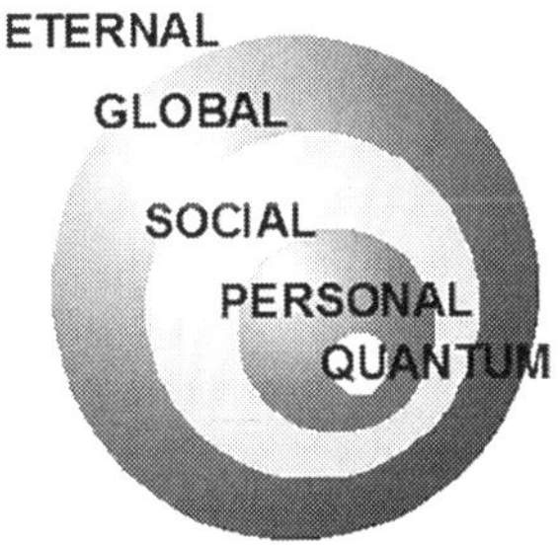

SPHERES of EXISTENCE

Since I had not yet moved from a head to a heart approach, I pursued a doctorate in holistic health sciences. I was compelled to understand and make sense of what had flowed into my awareness. This advanced training clarified a great deal and helped me to fine-tune the concepts within the *Blueprint*.

I was on a spiritual high with everything I had discovered. I wanted to share it but believed everyone would think I was a raving lunatic. I had no way to prove what I learned was true, so I remained a closet guru for a few years. Also, the *Blueprint* had grown so much that I did not have a clue how to present it in a way that would create the positive impact that I desired.

After struggling for six years to integrate what I learned into my way of being, I tried to share what I discovered through books and workshops. I had limited success until a life-changing meditation helped me to fully experience and integrate the *Blueprint* into my way of being.

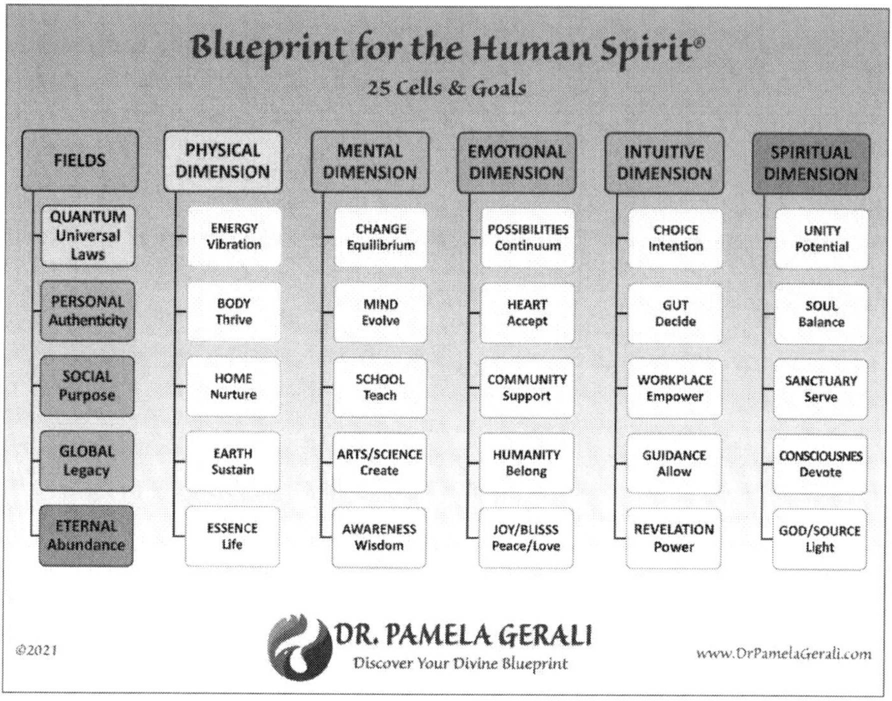

A New Way to Dance

On a balmy morning in October 2001, I experienced a life-changing meditation. During an hour and a half meditation, I relived an intensely dramatic event in fifteen past lives. There were children, men, and women from all walks of life, and they spanned the ages from ancient Mayan times to the early 1900s. Each one revealed a shift in consciousness relevant to our spiritual growth. See the Archetype chart on next page.

As I recorded their stories, I realized that the fifteen archetypes perfectly revealed how we evolve from helpless victims to ego-driven failures to conscious co-creators. The fact that there were fifteen primary boxes in the *Blueprint* matrix at that time is not a coincidence. Each past life mirrored exactly what one aspect of the *Blueprint* taught.

A few days later, a friend and therapist guided me back in time for a regression. I was a child at the feet of Jesus when he said, "Let the little children come to

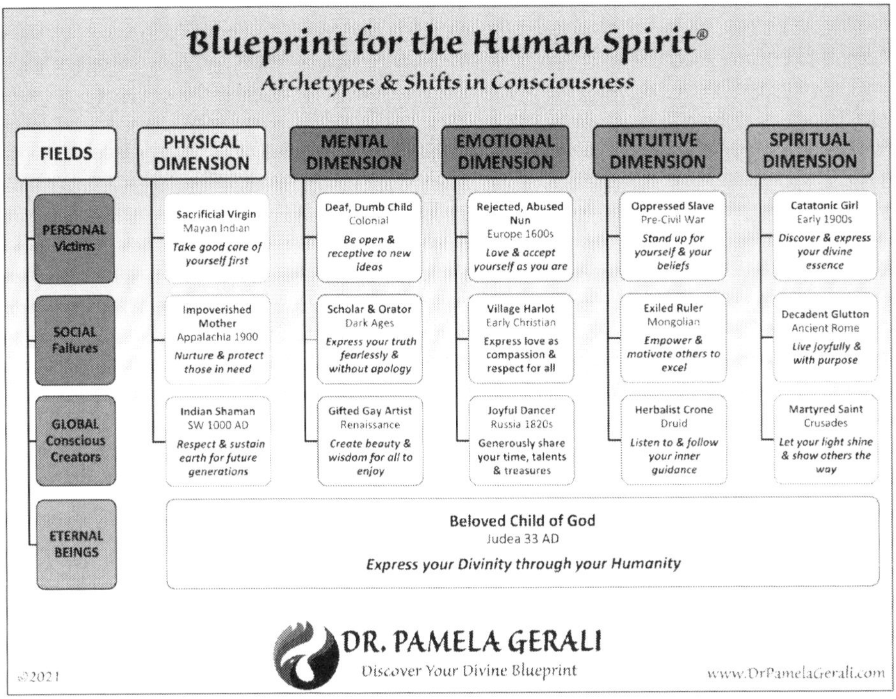

me, for theirs is the kingdom of heaven." This beloved child of God archetype represented the emerging eternal field of the *Blueprint*. It perfectly illustrated how we are the hands, heart, and voice of God on earth, and how we express our divinity through our humanity.

This meditation and regression transformed my life. From this moment on, the *Blueprint* was no longer just an interesting intellectual exercise. I deeply experienced and integrated its spiritual wisdom and practical guidance into my way of being. It was now a part of me. Finally, my head, heart, and soul merged into an integrated, synergistic whole. I was ready to dance, merging ego with essence.

More than a Performance

The *Blueprint for the Human Spirit* has changed my life from the inside out. I had shifted from left-brain dominance to an integrated head-heart-soul approach to life. I had left my career to become a spiritual seeker. As the *Blueprint* evolved, I healed old wounds and released fears that kept me from living authentically. Every dance step I learned brought me closer to the truth of my being.

While the *Blueprint* evolved, another amazing gift emerged. I discovered that I was highly intuitive, and a unique healing modality was gifted to me. I use psycho-spiritual mirroring, imagery, and muscle memory to reveal how your past and current life situations affect your body, beliefs, emotions, and spiritual awareness. This dramatic, interactive activation process guides you to experience shifts in perceptions so you can realize the truth of your being. With this gift of Spiritual Blueprinting, I have also healed wounds from my past so I can serve more compassionately and create more consciously.

Most importantly, on this amazing journey, I have discovered my higher purpose. I know that I am here now to put all the pieces together and share the *Blueprint* with the world. I realize that every life experience and choice has brought me to this moment. I am now ready and able to fulfill my sacred contract. The *Blueprint* and my Spiritual Blueprinting technique have evolved to the point where they are ready to share.

One amazing fact about the *Blueprint* is its universality. It is a dynamic tool for learning and increasing awareness for seekers of all faiths and walks of life. Since it contains universal truths that are compatible with ancient teachings, new science, Eastern philosophy, and Western psychology, it bridges the gap between religions and doctrines, cultures, and ages. It is relevant to and potentially helpful for individuals of all belief systems who are committed to their spiritual growth.

Words cannot express how grateful I am for these transformative experiences and gifts from Source. And the timing could not be more perfect. If the world needs anything right now, it is the *Blueprint.* This paradigm for conscious, and compassionate living can help transform what ails humanity. As we release victimhood, entitlement, and prejudice, we can all dance in harmony and realize our highest potential. Together we can change the world from the inside out.

Now that you are aware of how the *Blueprint* came to be and how it changed my life, I invite you will join me in this 40-day transforming dance where ego and essence merge. Let your divine diva out to dance and be all that you were born to be.

For more information about the *Blueprint for the Human Spirit,* visit my website: www.DrPamelaGerlai.com. You can watch a video about the Blueprint (www.DrPamelaGerali.com/blueprint/) or my transforming story, "Confessions of a Spiritually Promiscuous Woman" (Dr. Gerali Show - Unity of Venice (veniceunity.org). If you want more facts about the *Blueprint*, read the Q&A.

Day 1

From Discipline to Direction

One step, two steps, three steps; like winds of time experience joy of centuries, when movements become revelations of the dance of destinies.
– Shas Asad Rizvi

Confession:

I am undisciplined and resist the very thought of anything or anyone restricting me from doing what I want.

This is day one of a forty-day adventure into the depths of my soul. Where am I compelled to begin? With "DISCIPLINE!" Discipline and I do not have a particularly good relationship. I recall being punished quite harshly for disobeying my parents and not adhering to the rigid rules of their church. However, I certainly need a strong dose to follow through with my intentions. I have been guided and inspired to share my journey, to bare my soul by confessing anything and everything. This is an exercise in spiritual transparency where all will be revealed. As I remove layers of good intentions, wise utterings, and virtuous actions, I strip down to the bones of my being, down below all the pretenses and false impressions, to expose the real me. In the process, I hope to uncover my true Essence.

This will not be easy because Ego-Pamela wants everyone to think she is special, smart, and gifted. The process also will be challenging because for nearly two years I have drifted away from the habit of sitting in silence, meditating, and writing. In addition, I was a full-time caregiver for my husband during his many health challenges and surgeries. Every free moment was dedicated to projects for non-profit organizations. As a perpetual volunteer, I was addicted to the glowing compliments I received for sharing my creative talents and to the belief that I was indispensable.

Then the Universe intervened and stopped me in my tracks. I hit rock bottom when an energy-sapping health issue sent me to bed for nearly seven months. For a high-energy woman who typically operated at break-neck speed, this was a low blow. I was forced to let go of everything unessential in my life. I resigned from every team and project, backed out of every possible commitment, and delegated as many family obligations as possible. I sank into the comfort of my bed, read trashy novels, watched mindless movies, and ate comfort food. Chocolate, cupcakes, and cookies were my best friends. I gobbled up anything sweet for some much-needed energy, only to confirm that I am more than a little allergic to wheat, corn, and gluten. Instead of getting the desired burst of energy, I suffered from constant reflux, heartburn, joint aches, and lethargy.

Looking back, I am sure my body would have healed more quickly had I not been on a sugar binge and if I had tried some holistic healing measures. However, I lacked the discipline and focus. When I finally gave up and let go, relief came. My body healed and my energy was restored. I also discovered the desire and motivation to change my lifestyle. I spent the next six months eating right and exercising diligently. I am thrilled to report that I am back on track, ready to move forward, not just physically, but spiritually as well. A shift has occurred deep within, so I will pick up my pen and write once again. To do this will require even more dedication and discipline than I need to stay on the healthy bandwagon. Fortunately, I tapped into a source far beyond my limited capacity. I would never have been able to kick the sugar habit and lose over thirty pounds in four months without Divine Intervention and assistance.

Back to the topic of the day. Discipline and I have had a strained relationship. Mother used to stand me in the corner when I disobeyed. I would sob and stomp my feet trying to release the pent-up energy and frustration I experienced in this confined space. Twenty minutes was torture for a hyperactive child. Meditation still feels like a timeout as I struggle to be still and quiet the mind.

Punishment from Dad was more old school and usually involved an unpleasant reunion with the razor strap. My sisters and I were often disciplined for "sins" like wearing makeup, shortening our skirts, or cutting our hair. Our folks wanted to make sure we would not spend an eternity in hell and felt obligated to correct the errors of our ways.

No wonder I was deathly afraid as a child. House rules and church standards were so overwhelming, I knew I could never measure up. I could never be good enough to make it inside the pearly gates. We were doomed just for being born. I never understood the concept of original sin that hung like a black cloud over our heads. This misconception is one of many perpetuated by conservative religions. After all, how could a Heavenly Father damn his beloved children to a lake of fire? No loving parent would do that to his/her children. A devoted father would never abuse his children, even if correction were necessary.

Discipline is critical or I will squander away the rest of my life and never fulfill my higher purpose—to share the *Blueprint for the Human Spirit.* The unfinished books and projects in my computer confirm this fact. Without order, structure, and guidance, my very existence could be meaningless. I have received great insights through the *Blueprint* and am compelled to share them in unique ways. This is possible—if I embrace a disciplined lifestyle.

To fulfill my commitment to journal confessions for forty days, I will block out time in my schedule, sit in silence and prepare myself physically and spiritually to receive guidance. Then I will write what comes to me. My intention is to clear my soul and trust that others will be inspired as I expose my shortcomings. Through this process, I can also share revelations from the *Blueprint*, the amazing inner teacher that guided my awakening.

Once I have written in my journal, I will go to my antique secretary's desk and enter the message on my computer. Not long ago I realized my desk sits in a corner of my office. Am I punishing myself as Mother used to discipline me? I considered moving the furniture around, but the majestic view of cypress trees, birds of paradise, and bougainvillea in my back yard neutralizes negative memories of the corner. This perspective also offers moments of incredible inspiration. When a dragonfly lights gracefully on one of the flowers, I am reminded to release illusion and false pretenses so I can embrace truth. This is the intention of this forty-day journaling process.

The *Blueprint* revealed a great deal to me about discipline. As we internalize guidance from our parents, it transforms into self-discipline and positive direction. We make choices to create the structure needed to pursue our heart's desires and follow-through to their completion. Obviously, I still have a long way to go in the self-discipline arena. Without discipline and direction, I will never show up every day to complete this endeavor or tackle the many projects that I have abandoned.

Fortunately, I have one recent positive and remarkably successful experience with self-discipline. After an extended illness, I am back in shape and have regained my physical stamina. To achieve this goal, I eliminated gluten, sugar, and dairy from my diet and began a rigorous exercise program. With my new routine, a sense of order has graced my life. I am now ready to pick up my pen and live more productively and purposefully.

The word "discipline" stems from the Latin word for pupil or disciple. Isn't learning what this process is all about? I am a disciple of a healthy lifestyle and a dedicated student of spirituality. I am committed to this forty-day process to release old beliefs and patterns, exposing the true me. I am committed to dancing as PAMELA in capital letters—Essence, my higher, sacred self.

AFFIRMATION:

My life is disciplined and in harmony with Divine Order. I am One with All That Is.

DAY 2

From Scattered to Focused

Every day brings a chance for you to draw in a breath, kick off your shoes, and dance.
– Oprah Winfrey

CONFESSION:

I am easily pulled in different directions and struggle to remain focused on priorities.

After a few minutes of silence, my second confession quickly popped into my awareness—lack of attention. This challenge contributes to my less-than-stellar efforts to share the *Blueprint for the Human Spirit.* Unless I remain focused on this forty-day writing exercise, my intentions will also fall by the wayside. The many abandoned projects in my computer are a testament to the fact that without attention, I easily and quickly wander off course.

I recently spent four months working non-stop to create communication strategies and materials for a capital campaign for our church. True, it was extraordinarily successful, and I received the Very Important Volunteer award for my efforts, but this is a pattern. I genuinely want to remain focused on what is most important to me—my work with the *Blueprint.* There is nothing I want to do more than to share its spiritual wisdom and practical guidance. No one else has access to this information or has experienced its life-changing benefits.

I have many excuses for not remaining focused on my work. There are no deadlines as my work with the *Blueprint* is ongoing. I will never be finished because it is infinite in scope and continues to evolve as I grow in awareness. Although I have attempted to divide my activities into segments that I can complete in a reasonable timeframe, this has only produced limited results. I am also not accountable to anyone but myself. No one prods or pushes me, and I cannot always find the motivation from within. When an organization asks for my assistance, I have people to work with and timelines. The project is concrete and well defined. With these criteria, I efficiently and effectively finish the project.

My mind is like a busy bee that buzzes from flower to flower, collecting ideas and returning them to my computer-hive for storage. Before I can turn them into something sweet and appealing that will enrich the lives of others, I am compelled to chase after more nectar. It is a never-ending cycle. Each creative idea also begins small and doable, only to morph into a huge undertaking that demands more endurance and dedication than I can muster. I am a sprinter. I start at break-neck speed and peter out before reaching a distant goal.

My Higher Tea® project is a classic example. It began as a few words that ended in "ty" (spiritualiTea, creativiTea, responsibiliTea...). Then an outline for a book emerged, followed by the format for an ongoing women's group that had the potential to be replicated nationwide, complete with monthly programs, a blog, a training program, speaking engagements, etc. I was able to complete most of this goal but failed to continue marketing efforts to make it successful.

I have another excuse for not following through with my endeavors—I am not a maintenance gal. I am a creative spirit and prefer designing and developing new ideas. Once I shared an idea for a new initiative with my husband. I was extremely excited as I had an amazing dream and affirming vision about how this endeavor could uplift humanity. My insightful husband looked me straight in the eyes and asked if I were going to complete my current project first, or if I would be like my father who started many projects and never finished them.

WOW! This caught me by surprise. At the same time, I appreciated his honesty and the wake-up call. Obviously, I need to examine my work patterns and priorities. I am delighted that I inherited my father's creativity, but unlike him, I want to see my efforts mature to a point where they will benefit others. It is not easy for creative spirits to stay focused. Once an idea is revealed, verbalized, or written, it is out there and feels completed. Immediately, a new brainchild comes along and, like a sensual siren, it draws me down a new dance.

Now that I know why I have difficulty staying focused, I am determined to overcome this tendency. But how? Fortunately, my new morning ritual should help. I will rise early and go to my sacred space for meditation and writing. The first hour of the day is perfect because the atmosphere is free of demands, negativity, and interruptions. I pause in the Presence and consciously allow inspiration to flow for an hour. Then I take a half hour brisk walk with a friend and go to the Fitness Center or exercise at home. I enjoy a healthy shake, read the funnies for a dose of humor, and complete the daily Sudoku to sharpen my mind. When I return to work, I am so inspired and enthusiastic that I cannot wait to continue.

I will never forget my first experience with early rising. I was in the fourth grade and needed to study for a history test. Mother suggested I get up early and re-read the pertinent chapter in my textbook. As promised, she woke me up. Instead of staying with me, however, she went back to bed. I thought she was going to read the chapter to me, but NO! She abandoned me in the family room to study on my own. It was dark outside, and I was afraid and devastated. I could not stay focused long enough to read one paragraph at a time, even when I used my finger to keep place. I wasted most of that morning sobbing and feeling sorry for myself.

When we pay attention, the Universe has so much more to offer. We have so much to learn and enjoy. When not focused, we miss the tiger butterfly's elegant dance on the bougainvillea and the sweet melodies of the mockingbird outside the window. We miss the opportunity to learn from each encounter and overlook the abundance that Spirit provides. By focusing on goals or outcomes, we can also miss the glory of the moment and fail to enjoy the process of living in the present and Presence.

A few years ago, our family met in Ohio for a funeral during the winter. On our way back to the viewing following a quick meal, my husband took a wrong turn and drove a couple miles down a winding country road before he could make a U-turn. While he ranted and raved about poor directions, I looked out the window at the wonderland around us. Snow-laden pine trees glistened in the light of the full moon. I was enchanted with the sparkling beauty and exclaimed, "Look at the pretty trees!" Our daughters burst into laughter, assuming I was trying to diffuse the tense situation with a little humor. I was in the moment, totally focused on the exquisite scene. Now when a family member starts complaining about a negative situation, we tell them to look at the pretty trees. It is a perfect reminder to live in the Now and enjoy what is.

I am thankful for the guidance I have received to date. Without greater focus I may not be able to complete this forty-day project. By affirming my intention and remaining committed to my new routine, I know I can do this. I practice saying "No" to those who ask for help so I can remain focused on the *Blueprint*—my priority. I remain true to my Self and avoid distractions. I will complete this project and tackle other viable ventures that have been abandoned, but only if they are compatible with my higher purpose. It is now easy and effortless, and I am enjoying the process.

Affirmation:

I pay attention every moment and remain focused on divinely guided priorities. I am true to my higher purpose and myself. I eliminate everything unessential in my life.

DAY 3

From Aimless to Purposeful

Dance and sing to your music. Embrace your blessings. Make today worth remembering.
– Steve Mariboli

CONFESSION:

I struggle to remain purposeful even though I am aware of my higher calling.

Discipline and focus are great, but without purpose—without a goal, mission, or meaning—they are useless. I have known since 1995 what my higher purpose is. I am here now, commissioned by a higher authority, to share the *Blueprint for the Human Spirit* with the world. This divinely inspired matrix guided me out of a spiritual void into a state of greater awareness. I was transformed, one concept at a time, as the *Blueprint* evolved in harmony with my awakening.

To remain true to one's reason for being is easier said than done. I do my best to live in harmony with the *Blueprint's* revelations, embracing and expressing them through my thoughts, words, and deeds. However, my best intentions are not enough. It is often easier to abandon my goals and join those around me. I waste time in the evenings watching TV with my husband. He likes detective shows with all their intensity, drama, and gore. I would rather watch heart-warming Hallmark movies with their sweet, predictable, non-violent love stories.

The fact that I am easily swayed is the first of many reasons why I am not diligent in sharing the *Blueprint.* Another reason is its complexity. I have no idea how or where to start. The *Blueprint* also continues to evolve as my understanding deepens. Initially, I only had an intellectual, superficial grasp of its wisdom. After living with it and fully experiencing its powerful truths, I now view it from a more profound, metaphysical, and mystical perspective. Instead of interpreting the words literally, I sense their underlying meaning in my bones.

Another reason for not following through on my unique purpose is that I am unclear how to proceed. I published *Higher Tea: The Essence of Joy*, an introduction to the *Blueprint*, but have at least six other books in various stages of completion. They include a text with details on each aspect of the matrix; a sequel to my first book, *Higher Tea for the Thirsty Soul*; a humorous ranting in Erma Bombeck style entitled, *If the World is an Oyster, Where are my Pearls?*; book of poetry, *inner nature*, which I would like to integrate with my husband's photos…

In addition to writing, I absolutely love facilitating workshops, speaking at churches, giving keynote presentations, and doing intuitive healings. The *Blueprint* is the basis for all these activities, but I am less than effective in promoting my work. This confessions project is related to a performance that includes music, PowerPoint, dance, and audience participation. The options are truly infinite. I honestly do not know where or how to continue. I know how to start, but I have not been able to follow through on my exhaustive menu of inspired and empowering ideas. I do not know what to tackle first, second, or third. HELP!

Another challenge is my tendency to focus on the process while the purpose driving my efforts takes a back seat. The original basis for my creative endeavors—to share wisdom and practical guidance from the *Blueprint*—can be diluted or abandoned while planning and implementing a program. At least I know my reason for being, Ego-Pamela boasts, so I am one quantum leap ahead of the clueless.

Once, when I felt quite smug about having nailed my higher purpose, I asked my husband if he knew his. Before revealing his answer, I will share that he was an extraordinarily successful businessman, and now that he is retired, he enjoys photography and golfing with his buddies. Regarding my inquiry, he quickly responded with a resounding "Yes. I am here to support you so you can fulfill your higher purpose." When I retrieved my jaw from the floor, I hugged him, and with tears of gratitude in my eyes, thanked him for being in my life. In that moment, I was reminded once again of how perfect the Universe works. It has provided me with everything I need to live purposefully—the perfect mate, unlimited resources, divine guidance, and support of many sacred sisters.

I am not afraid of failure, nor do I fear success. I have the talent to do what is required, so what is my real excuse? Maybe I am just lazy. Is it possible I do not want to work hard enough to succeed? I could so easily take myself off the hook and squander away the rest of my life as a retiree, but a supernatural force is pulling me forward.

To share the *Blueprint* will require a great deal of effort and devotion. It will demand more energy, enthusiasm, and endurance than I have been able to sustain in the past. Am I strong enough? Yes, I am! In fact, a friend confirmed this in a joint healing last week. But don't you have extreme energy swings, my Inner Weakling warns. Right now, I have more than enough energy, Essence replies. True. In the past I rode the waves in an all-or-none mode, knowing the tide would soon ebb. While cruising at break-neck speed, I accomplished a great deal only to crash into a state of inactivity for a mandatory time of recovery. Fortunately, a healthier lifestyle has restored my physical strength and stamina, eliminating one more potential block.

Ego counters with a new and very clever strategy: "Instead of a higher purpose, perhaps your desires are only an ego entrapment. Have you received the *Blueprint* purely to raise your own awareness?"

"Perhaps true," Essence replies. "To hoard and hide something so amazing is not congruent with who I am. Somewhere between pride and false humility is a place where amazing things come to life." I pause to observe the inner debate, wondering if this is another stalling tactic and more justification for my lack of progress.

Perhaps I am afraid of my own power and potential. Marian Williamson shared insight on this in her book, *A Return to Love*. "Our deepest fear is not that we are inadequate. Our deepest fear is that we are powerful beyond measure." I believe I am empowered enough to embrace a divinely guided, purposeful life. I am not the shy, quiet, or insecure person I was as a teen. Maybe a publicist could help move my creative expressions out of my office and into the world. Then again, perhaps all I need is to focus.

When we live on purpose, we grace the planet with our presence. The lives of others improve through our conscious, loving expressions. The time for being wishy-washy is over. I will honor what I have learned and be a living example of these universal truths. I will quit making excuses and renew my commitment to live with purpose. Discipline and focus will help. And I will no longer rely so heavily on Ego-Pamela to make this happen. I will allow the infinite, all-knowing, all-powerful Spirit to express through me in brilliant and beautiful ways.

Affirmation:

I embrace my unique purpose and let my light radiantly shine in loving and meaningful ways to uplift humanity.

Day 4

From Vacillation to Perseverance

I don't want people who want to dance, I want people who have to dance.
– George Balanchine

Confession:

When things get tough, I take the easy route or pursue something else instead of persevering.

Whenever the word perseverance comes to mind, I think of my father. He had his own word for it, "stickability." Although he preferred the creative phase and he abandoned projects before they were completed, he encouraged others to stay the course. His favorite poem, which was by Edgar Albert Guest, was about perseverance.

> *"Somebody said that it couldn't be done, but he with a chuckle replied, that maybe it couldn't but he would be one that wouldn't say so 'til he tried. So he buckled right in with a bit of a grin on his face; if he worried he hid it and tackled the thing that couldn't be done and he did it."*

Dad lost his right hand in a sawmill accident at age nineteen and wore a hook. Instead of feeling sorry for himself, he discovered that he could do a great deal with his artificial limb beside scaring our dates and entertaining kids as

Captain Hook. He designed special attachments for different tasks. One had a hammer to help with his construction business. Another held a bow for archery hunting—he always got a deer. Losing a limb would not stop him!

A cardinal became one of Dad's greatest adversaries. It tapped on the window at its reflection each morning and disrupted morning devotions. Dad tried everything to stop the incessant noise, but nothing worked until he strung fishing line back and forth across the deck so the birds could not reach the window. His ingenuity overcame adversity.

On the first Father's Day after my dad passed, I called Mother and told her that I was thinking of him while making plans to attend an upcoming reunion for his mother's family. During our conversation, I heard a tapping on my office window. The sound became so intense I went to the window and discovered a cardinal hovering at eye-level on the other side of the glass. Dad was making his presence known! I said, "It's a cardinal! It's Dad!" The fact that he chose Father's Day to say "Hi" in this special way was no coincidence. Talk about perseverance!

Exactly one year after dad died, my blood pressure became critically elevated, and I had to go to the ER. I had tried everything possible to bring it down—meditation, acupuncture, massage, exercise, deep breathing, better nutrition, less stress—but nothing helped. Since Dad had many strokes due to uncontrolled hypertension, I knew I was also at risk.

When I was escorted to a bed in the ER, I looked up and saw two cardinals painted on the ceiling above me. Thanks to a creativity project, patients, family members, doctors, and hospital staff had painted ceiling tiles. It was not a coincidence that my space was graced with the powerful symbolism of cardinals. They represent transformation and awakening, as well as expressing and integrating truth. Thanks to a little help from Dad, our feathered friends, and a commitment to a healthier lifestyle, my blood pressure is now under control.

Day 4

Transformation and conscious living require perseverance because they usually do not occur spontaneously. We first become aware of an idea and notice it a few times before experiencing it at a deep, personal level. Unless we grasp the scope and breadth of its subtle nuances, then fully embrace and integrate it into our routine, we will not awaken.

This is how the *Blueprint* evolved one step at a time. Each vague notion was seeded in my awareness, then sprouted into an inspired idea that grew until it blossomed and was fully integrated into my way of being. One divine idea at a time, it emerged from a word or thought into an impression that I noticed in my surroundings. My senses kicked into action as I became increasingly aware of its presence or absence in the world around me. Friends and family mirrored the attitudes and actions associated with each concept. They helped me learn and integrate new beliefs into my way of being.

Here is a classic example: as I explored the idea of overlapping energies, I noticed how affected I was by my husband's emotional state. While driving, either he is in a hurry and yells at other drivers to get out of his lane, or he drives like a retired grandpa and tries to get more than fifty miles per gallon from his Prius wagon. He seems to putt along when I am in a hurry.

As I became more conscious of how his attitude affected mine, I shared what I had learned about the benefits of going with the flow. Of course, that went over as well as me telling him that he didn't own the road! Today I am more inclined to diffuse negativity with humor. Instead of preaching or joking, I try to remember to look at myself in the rear-view mirror. I need to accept what is and not react. This continues to be one of my greatest challenges and my husband just reflects it! I may have learned a great deal, but still have light-years to go!

The dictionary defines perseverance as adherence to a course of action or purpose and being steadfast in beliefs. Perseverance is critical for this forty-day exercise. It is also necessary to honor my intentions to live purposefully. With my new morning ritual, it now seems effortless, but this is just the beginning. How will I feel after a week, or ten or twenty days? Will it continue to be easy to knuckle down and complete a re-write? I am not sure, but at this moment, I am excited, eager to wake up and see what Spirit has in store. I am in the flow—divinely inspired.

If my father and others could stay the course despite seemingly insurmountable challenges, so can I. I can muster the necessary discipline to remain focused on my purpose and follow through on my commitment to share the *Blueprint*. With an open heart and mind, inspiration will flow and will effortlessly create materials and programs that are simple, effective, and enjoyable. Albert Einstein said, "If you can't explain it simply, you don't understand it well enough." I would add that if you cannot make it interesting and fun, don't bother!

Not all lessons are easy, but I will continue to welcome them all—the painful and the pleasant. I will embrace each step toward greater awareness because it is more about the journey than the destination. For each opportunity to learn and grow I am profoundly grateful. I almost said, "Bring it on!" but I would rather that lessons be less dramatic and traumatic than they have been in the past. Instead, I will affirm that I quickly grasp the spirit of the lessons and integrate changes into my way of being, so I no longer require cosmic whacks to get unstuck. Regardless of the outcome, I will persevere and follow divine guidance.

AFFIRMATION:

I persevere and remain true to my higher purpose, knowing everything I need is being provided.

DAY 5

From Bingeing to Healthy Eating

To live is to be musical, starting with the blood dancing in your veins. Everything living has a rhythm. Do you feel your music?
– Michael Jackson

CONFESSION:

Instead of eating in a healthy manner, I am addicted to sugar and am a closet sweets junkie.

One of my earliest memories of Dad is a day when I was making breakfast with him. I was five and Mother was in the hospital after giving birth to my youngest sister. I stood on a chair by the sink as we made hot chocolate with an extra spoonful of sugar, and toast with mountains of grape jelly—just the way I liked them. No wonder I have a sweet tooth. No wonder I was hyperactive!

I have always liked sweets. I remember eating cookie dough by the heaping spoonful around the holidays. While I was in college, I began mixing little batches of brownies, chocolate chip cookies, or sugar cookies in coffee mugs. I ate it raw or baked them in the microwave, depending on my mood. But I always snuck bites when no one was watching. Instead of hiding this unhealthy habit for years, I should have packaged the idea and made a fortune.

I have finally given up this sugary pastime and for six months have been in a healthy eating mode—no gluten, sugar, or dairy. Combined with an ambitious exercise regimen, the pounds have melted away. This time I am determined to reach my goal and stay in shape. Enough with the yo-yoing! I have gone up and down more times than I can count in the past thirty-five years. Unfortunately, the pounds increased with each birthday and every year it became more challenging to take off the extra weight.

Now, after being gluten-free for a few months, my labs have significantly improved. My thyroid levels are back to normal after being low for years. My blood sugar also dropped fifteen points. It had slowly climbed with my weight to the highest possible level that could still be considered "within normal limits." I also feel much better. I no longer have heartburn, reflux, abdominal pain, or itchy skin. These excellent results have reinforced my incentive to continue a healthy routine.

Regardless of my best intentions, I am still tempted to fall off the "Sugar-free" wagon when my energy wanes. Last winter, when I was down with viral thyroiditis, I could not get enough cookies and candy. I craved and consumed a bushel of sweets, hoping they would bolster my sagging energy. But NO! To be honest, they most likely drained my vitality even more and slowed the healing process.

Now when I need an energy boost, I have a few raw nuts or fruit. Occasionally Pammy Sue, the needy little girl who craves some sugar from her daddy, will come out to play. No amount of self-discipline will stop her from diving face-first into a vat of chocolate. She overrides all rational thought and reasoning ability.

Since I am being honest, I might as will clear my soul of the residual guilt from yesterday's indulgence. I will preface my confession with a good excuse: I was exhausted by hours of driving and intense time with family.

My day began with a healthy shake for breakfast, then another for lunch, which I enjoyed on a boring three-hour drive. I nibbled on some pecans and grapes, but the closer I came to my destination, the weaker I felt. At the Service

Plaza, I avoided the fast-food counter, but did not make it past the vending machines before Pammy Sue showed up. She bought a bag of Peanut M&Ms and justified her purchase since they contain whole nuts. Unfortunately, they did not satisfy her craving.

After I checked into the hotel and made a second trip to the desk because the key card would not open my room, I was cooked. I needed something, *anything* for a jolt of energy. Since the sugar I consumed earlier had not helped, I bought chicken tenders at a nearby fast-food restaurant. Feeling slightly better, I visited my niece and her three darling children, then went to my brother's home for his youngest daughter's second birthday celebration. I was extremely glad I had a snack because we did not eat until after 8:00. This was extremely late for me since my husband and I typically have our evening meal between 5:30 and 6:30.

When the birthday girl finally opened her gifts, it was 9:30. I wanted to leave, but the kids begged me to read a bedtime story. One story turned into three, one for each of them. Then there were dishes to wash and repeated hugs for the kiddies who wanted me to spend the night. NOT A CHANCE! Although I love these delightful children, I am not used to the noise and commotion. As I headed for the door, I heard someone mention the possibility of baking a birthday cake. It was after 10:00 so I kept walking.

What did I do when I dragged my weary self into the hotel? Headed straight to the vending machine for a Snickers bar! The last thing I heard as I was leaving my brother's home was "birthday cake," so Pammy Sue's sweet tooth was triggered. Do I feel guilty? A little. Will this slip permanently knock me off my healthy regimen? Not this time.

Today I will drive back to my comfortable life with my amazing husband and a life free of confusion and conflict. Fortunately, my morning routine was not broken even though I was out of town. Without setting my alarm, I awoke before 6:00 to meditate and write. I spent some time on the exercise machines in the hotel fitness room, then had fruit and hard-boiled eggs for breakfast.

The do-it-yourself waffles that flood the lobby with their siren's smell will not tempt me.

I am incredibly grateful that my husband has also embraced my healthy lifestyle. He gratefully eats what I prepare and does not complain. If I do not feel like cooking or if we had a big lunch, he is perfectly happy with a healthy shake for dinner. He has also benefited from a diet free of gluten, dairy, and sugar. Although he is unable to exercise due to a bad back, he has lost over twenty pounds. It is not fair that I have had to work so hard and exercise like a maniac every day to get in shape, while he does it just sitting around!

I will keep my commitment to a healthy lifestyle despite occasional temptations that arise. At the same time, I know little indulgences like dark chocolate are OK and will not set me back. I have learned from experience that an all-or-none approach does not work and neither does dieting. Diets are temporary fixes and have contributed to my weight swings. They have not helped me stay in balance. Now that I am on track, I can enjoy the permanent benefits of a healthy lifestyle—an ample supply of vitality and stamina. I am confident that I will have more than enough energy and perseverance to remain true to my higher purpose.

Affirmation:

I nourish my body with whole, natural food so I can enjoy abundant health and energy to realize my higher purpose.

DAY 6

From Illness to Wellness

Our biological rhythms are the symphony of the cosmos, music embedded deep within us to which we dance, even when we can't name the tune.
– Deepak Chopra

CONFESSION:

This Nurse and Doctor of Holistic Health Sciences isn't always in perfect health or able to heal herself.

I grew up in a small town with minimal access to the outside world. Since we did not have a TV, my perspective on career options were limited—housewife (not a chance), secretary (not for this independent thinker), teacher, or nurse. A job opportunity broke the tie, and my journey as a healer began with a certified nursing assistant course. Within two weeks after starting the program, I knew I wanted to be a nurse and applied to the University of Pittsburgh. I registered for classes one week later and the rest is history. I loved caring for patients. In typical high-energy mode, I efficiently and compassionately ensured they were comfortable and received everything needed to restore wellness.

Volunteer work with the American Cancer Society and the Oncology Nursing Society opened doors to organizational work. This encouraged me to pursue a graduate degree in Public Health. One promotion at a time, I climbed the corporate ladder and enjoyed a fulfilling, meaningful career. My expertise was in program planning and implementation, which offered excellent opportunities to share my creativity.

While an executive at Prevent Blindness America, I attended the Center for Creative Leadership in Greensboro, NC. This fabulous program introduced me to visioning, journaling, and thinking outside the box. A huge, conversion-like shift occurred within, and I started down a spiritual path. Four months later when my job no longer seemed in harmony with my new focus, I walked away. Although I believed my decision was best at the time, it was not easy to let go of the title, salary, and satisfaction of helping others. My position and career had been my focus and identity for so long, I felt lost without them. However, now I had plenty of time to read and study about spirituality and alternative healing.

The first time I experienced a non-traditional healing was with a cervical polyp. My gynecologist had diagnosed the problem and confirmed its presence with ultrasound. My older sister, a student of spirituality and alternative healing, guided me to a sacred inner place where my body took over and healed itself. Without any intention or interference on my part, I pushed on my abdomen. I knew intuitively where to push, how long to push, and how hard to push. Two weeks later, I passed the benign polyp. My doctor was amazed that I no longer needed a procedure. I was thrilled and wanted to know more.

As I opened my heart and mind to the *Blueprint for the Human Spirit*, a new form of healing emerged. When I prayed for people, my body went into motion. I saw images and moved energy around to eliminate negativity and release blocks. I had no idea what was happening at the time, but it made more sense as I explored intuitive and psychic healing strategies. This amazing ability evolved until I am now able to sit opposite someone or be with them on the phone, close my eyes, sense the Presence of God, and affirm our receptivity.

Throughout the sessions, I speak in first person about the images I sense, and describe what my motions and positions mean. Issues are revealed with shifts in perception or techniques that can resolve them. Hidden mental attitudes, emotional problems, and spiritual concerns are brought to light and transformed by truth. One at a time, challenges are uncovered and clients experience release and transformation. Some healings target issues from the past, while others address the present or future concerns. I call this healing process Spiritual Blueprinting.

Unlike typical medicine, which focuses on symptoms and curing disease, my intuitive approach addresses underlying issues that can cause or manifest as physical disorders. If these are ignored, permanent health will not be realized. Disease will recur and patients will never experience wellness and wholeness. Although I embrace alternative healing, I believe integrated medicine—merging the best of both worlds—can be most effective. When we work together for the highest good of the whole patient, they will thrive.

Many people wonder if I can perform healings on myself. The answer is sometimes, but not always. Years ago, I suffered with a painful muscle spasm in my upper back. I tried everything to release it—massage, heat, chiropractic, over-the-counter pain meds, stretching—but nothing worked. It could not have occurred at a more inopportune time. Our house was being painted so everything was boxed and in a state of disarray. Friends were staying with us after being evacuated for a hurricane that was headed for their home. My husband was out of commission with painful back issues and our daughter was recovering from extensive knee surgery. She needed a great deal of assistance, so I was her full-time physical therapist, daily care assistant, laundress, chef, chauffeur, entertainer, etc.

When I awoke with severe discomfort at three in the morning, I sat holding my head in my hands and said aloud, “Help me!” A voice responded, “You do healings, don’t you?” Yes! I took a deep breath, let go, and tapped into that divine source of loving energy. I went through a series of scenes that clearly revealed how I had given away my power and lacked the ability to say “No” to the demands of others. Only by shifting my perception could I say “Yes” to that which was in my highest good. I experienced firsthand the benefits of non-resistance, of allowing. The many monkeys on my back that presented as painful muscle spasms scurried away and have never returned.

A great deal of pressure comes with a Doctorate in Holistic Health Sciences and the ability to perform intuitive healings. Healers are expected to prevent illnesses, cure diseases, sense when anything bad is going to happen, and know how to avoid unpleasantness. Perhaps these impressions arise from my own perfectionistic tendencies and guilt from my Inner Critic. Regardless, shame hangs over my head like a black cloud whenever I become sick.

Last winter I was incapable of healing myself and did not even try. I lacked the necessary attention, energy, and connection. Did I feel guilty for getting sick? Yes! As a metaphysician, my Inner Critic insisted I should have been able to stay healthy. It reminded me that we create health or illness by our thoughts, beliefs, and actions. Did I feel guilty about not being able to heal myself? Of course! My Inner Critic demands to know how I can help others if I cannot help myself. Fortunately, I have learned to tune out this negativity and no longer buy into metaphysical guilt.

When I finally recovered and had enough energy to resume my practice, I received a call from the woman who obtained a gift certificate for a healing that I had donated to a charity auction. Since I had been out of commission for almost a year, I experienced a flicker of doubt. I was not sure if I was ready but took the risk and scheduled a session. All I could do was trust and try. It worked! I am thrilled to be back on track, not only with my own health, but also with my ability to serve others. For this amazing gift from our abundant Universe, I am most grateful.

Affirmation:

I open my awareness and follow divine guidance to maintain wellness and bring healing to others and myself.

DAY 7

From Falsehood to Truth

There is…a time to weep and a time to laugh, a time to mourn and a time to dance.
– Ecclesiastes 3:4

CONFESSION:

I avoid confrontation and tell little white lies to protect myself from criticism and to avoid hurting people's feelings.

The New Testament says that the truth shall set you free. Well, the truth got me punished when I was young, so I learned to lie. Negative reinforcement trained me to be dishonest. As a child, I was not permitted to disagree with my parents, teachers, or other authority figures. Differing opinions were considered disobedience or willfulness, and neither was tolerated. I learned to say "Yes" whether I agreed or not. I was compliant, and kept my mouth closed and my thoughts, ideas, and beliefs to myself. I was little Miss Goody-Two-Shoes, the sweet daughter who appeared to never disobey or get into trouble. It is interesting that Pamela means "sweetness." Having made a commitment to transparency, I must admit that I was just smart enough not to get caught.

While a teen, I also kept my older sister out of trouble. I was her protector. Our parents were extremely hard on her, expected her to disobey, and assumed she was guilty with or without evidence. If Mother or Dad asked for my sister, and if there was even a remote possibility that she was with the boy they had forbidden her to see, I ran the hills to find her. I did my best to make sure she was home before our folks became suspicious.

I also took on the role of family mediator without even realizing what I was doing. Despite my best intentions to keep the peace, I did not always succeed and sometimes paid the price. As an eighteen-year-old college student, I came home one evening and walked in on a family disagreement. A younger sister did not want to wear an outfit my mother had made for her. Dad insisted she wear it and told me to tell her she looked fine in it. I should explain that until we graduated from high school, Mother sewed our clothes and dressed us alike. We looked like we belonged to a conservative girls' school in our long dresses with sleeves below the elbows. To top it off, Mother usually had a matching dress. You can imagine how humiliated we felt as teenagers. We could not express our personalities. We literally had no identity since no one could tell us apart!

Back to the story. With all the diplomacy I had developed by that young age, I complimented Mother on her efforts, but acknowledged my sister's preference. Obviously, Dad did not like my tactful response and slapped me across the face. This was the first time I expressed an opinion different from my folks, so he obviously was surprised. I did not say a word, but went to my room, closed the door, packed a small suitcase, and hid it under my bed. I tried to study for a final exam the next day but was too upset. Later Dad came to my room and berated me even more for criticizing my mother. I remained silent.

The next morning after my final exam, I drove a hundred miles to where my boyfriend was attending college. I called home later in the afternoon and told Mother where I was. When Dad got on the line, I hung up. Three days later, I returned home in time to take another exam, and when I arrived, my father apologized. This was the first and only time he ever said, "I am sorry" to me.

Day 7

Today's topic was not a surprise. No doubt, it has something to do with the tickle in my throat. Years ago, I had one sore throat after another, often when I was supposed to perform. I studied voice and was an excellent singer but was afraid I would make a mistake. A sore throat ensured that I would not fail, as I did not have to sing.

I now know that the throat chakra has everything to do with expression. When I avoid speaking my truth, the unspoken words stick in my craw and irritate my throat until I literally get a cold. So why now, why today? Perhaps because I was bone tired after a trip across the state. When I am exhausted, my throat is also vulnerable. On the other hand, I may have failed to honestly express my views on a potentially serious issue regarding my nephew. I will take some Echinacea and vitamin C, get additional rest, and affirm that I am healthy and whole.

During the past twenty years, I have studied many masters and dabbled in numerous spiritual practices. I was concerned that I would be tempted to follow false teachings, but this did not stop me. I prayed that I would know "truth" when I heard or saw it. When the *Blueprint* began to emerge, it felt right, but I had no proof or data to support it. All I had to rely on was my own anecdotal experiences. Ego-driven Pamela craved evidence that she was right, and the *Blueprint* could change the world and the lives of everyone in it.

Despite my best intentions, I am not always successful at integrating what I have learned. When I cannot walk my talk, I feel like a fraud. Since I have written a spiritual book, speak at churches and do healings, integrity is expected. I know that the core of my being is Essence and that I am never separate from truth or God. Perhaps this forty-day exercise in Self-discovery will help me fully embrace the truth of who I AM and learn to express it every moment of every day. Confirmation from my gut indicates that, after a week of soul searching, I have finally figured out the purpose of this challenge. I will continue to peel away the layers of fear and doubt, guilt, and shame, one memory at a time. I will dig beneath the façade to reveal my Higher Self.

When I am spiritually naked, stripped of old beliefs and false pretenses, I will recognize the God within.

In the meantime, I will carefully observe my actions and make sure they are in agreement with what I know to be true. I will follow Spirit's guidance to ensure that I openly and compassionately express truth and live in alignment with Essence. When not in truth, stress complicates our lives. Only by bringing action into alignment with knowing will we find inner peace and the joy it brings. Only then can we dance in harmony with our authentic Self.

AFFIRMATION:

I embrace Essence, the truth of my being and compassionately express my divinity through my humanity.

DAY 8

From Perfectionism to Perfectly Imperfect

The first dance is the worst dance; the last dance is the best dance! All the roads of persistent practice lead to the Land of Perfection.
–Mehmet Murat Ildan

CONFESSION:

Nothing I do seems good enough; no matter how hard I try, I will never be perfect.

For years, I have struggled to be good enough and do everything well enough. The preacher told us repeatedly that we were sinners, condemned because of Original Sin. Church members scrutinized us according to a list of "standards" a mile long. We could not breathe for fear we would do it wrong and never make it inside the pearly gates. Since spending an eternity in a lake of fire was not an acceptable option, we did our best to be flawless. We tried to do what was right but could never measure up.

Our folks raised my sisters and me according to the outmoded commandment that "little girls are to be seen and not heard." This meant we had to keep our mouths closed and look perfect to make a positive impression. To be or do anything less would reflect poorly on our parents. When combined with the many religious standards on outward appearance, this was impossible. How could we be the picture of loveliness in identical granny dresses without makeup or jewelry? My three sisters and I attracted a lot of attention, not because we were gorgeous, but because Mother dressed us alike. People did a double take because they thought they were seeing quadruple.

I worked hard to please everyone and perform my chores to the best of my ability. However, I never felt complimented or encouraged. For years, my sisters and I mowed the lawns of our grandparents, great uncle, the elderly neighbors, and the parsonage. Never once did we receive a "thank you" or a quarter for our efforts. We did what we were told, when we were told, and did not complain. When Dad tried to teach me something and I asked for feedback, he would say, "Gettin' there." Instead of realizing I had performed the job well enough, or that I had learned what I needed, I thought that I was being told, "Not good enough!" This made me try even harder.

One of my sisters was encouraged to draw a symbolic picture of our family for a psych class. She drew a car with me in the backseat looking out the window with the label "Picture Perfect Pamela." At first glance, one might think I live a charmed life while the rest of my family thrives on chaos. I completed advanced education and excelled in my career. I am happily married to a successful man—I finally got it right after a bad marriage and a few rotten relationships. We have a lovely home, travel, and enjoy each other's company. I have nothing to worry about except my husband's health issues.

The truth is I have made different choices than my siblings. They have generously given me forty nieces and nephews. I never had children, but am blessed with two stepdaughters, a granddaughter and three great-grandbabies. The main reason I decided not to have children is I believed I could not be a perfect parent and enjoy a successful career at the same time. I believed my work would be more fulfilling than being a full-time homemaker and mother. In addition, I did not want to be as strict as my parents were. Since I was very tough on myself, this was a distinct possibility.

If my parents were demanding and critical, I became my own worst enemy as an adult. I set the standard so high, I could never measure up. No doubt this compelled me to be the best, to finish first, and stay on top. I set ambitious goals and tackled them with dogged determination. Nothing got in my way since my relentless Inner Critic demanded perfection.

While I was the Program Director for a nationwide organization, I oversaw a special project. The deadline for product distribution was fast approaching. I did my best to stay focused and complete it on time. I failed to notice that my assistant was pregnant, had morning sickness, and was concerned about her future. I may have excelled in project planning, but obviously lacked people skills. In fact, if the organization wanted the best program with innovative ideas and exceptional materials completed on time and within budget, I was in charge. If they wanted everyone to be happy with the process, someone else was selected. Apparently, I was as tough on others as I was on myself.

A life-changing program at the Center for Creative Leadership brought this to light and helped me to change my ways. I began listening more attentively and interacting more effectively with colleagues and staff. I removed the blinders that kept me from seeing what was happening beyond the narrow scope of the latest project. I also became more tuned in to and supportive of my staff. My husband might disagree because when I am in a work mode, I fail to notice when he comes into my office. If the reason for his visit is important, I am sure he will be more persistent!

I believe the Universe has provided everything I need to live up to my potential and fulfill my higher purpose. I have no excuse for not working diligently and doing everything in my power to share the *Blueprint.* So why do I have an office full of abandoned projects? Beside the fact that I have difficulty staying focused, I do not believe they are quite good enough to share with the world. My perfectionistic tendencies have become the ultimate excuse. I sometimes need to trick myself by scheduling a presentation or workshop to complete my latest brainchild. Occasionally friends help by insisting I implement a seminar and share my latest insights.

The *Blueprint for the Human Spirit* is my baby. My Higher Power commissioned me to give birth to this inspired guide. Through journaling, contemplation, and meditation, this gift is maturing. I hope that I have evolved to the point where I can eloquently and effectively share its sacred truths. If I work both day and night until I make my transition, I still could not do enough to impart all its sacred revelations. However, as Don Miguel Ruiz encourages us in his book, *The Four Agreements*, we can only do our best every moment. I now know that our best is good enough.

I realize my quest for perfection is ego-driven, misguided, and has blocked my potential. I know that I am perfectly imperfect—a beloved child of God—just like everyone else. I no longer believe I am less capable, nor do I need confirmation to prove my efforts are worthwhile. As I move forward on my spiritual path, I embrace my sacred contract and pursue my life's work with enthusiasm. It is how I express my divinity. I let go of all expectations to be perfect because Essence already is. At the same time, I thank my Inner Critic who pushed me to learn as much as possible, develop my creative talents, and strive for excellence. These qualities have served me well and will continue to do so as I share spiritual wisdom and practical guidance from the *Blueprint*.

AFFIRMATION:

I am a beloved child of God and do my best to express my true divine nature every moment of every day.

Day 9

From Instability to Balance

Life is short and there will always be dirty dishes, so let's dance.
– James Howe

Confession:

I struggle to find balance in my life with extreme energy swings and a tendency to operate in an all-or-nothing mode.

A few days ago, I confessed that in the past I experienced extreme energy highs and lows. More often than not, I was flying. However, when I ran out of steam, I crashed. I hesitated to schedule anything far into the future, fearing it would fall in the middle of a low spell. Lows are incredibly challenging to someone who typically has a lot of energy, but I learned to adapt. I had no choice. Instead of resisting and berating myself, I rested. I rode the waves and tried to honor my body's need for a break.

I recently discovered a major contributing factor to these swings—gluten. I knew I was sensitive to wheat and corn but did not realize how deeply they affected me. When I eliminated gluten from my diet, my energy became very stable. Now I am vivacious and no longer need to budget my activities to make sure I have enough energy to sustain me throughout the day. I can get up at six, exercise intensely, write or work at my desk for three or four hours, golf, prepare meals, run errands, and still have enough steam to last through the early evening. Since gluten also affects the thyroid, I am pleased to have this gland in balance as well.

I must also confess that I have been as off and on with my work as I have been in the physical realm. When inspiration flowed and my stamina was above average, I worked non-stop until I collapsed. I was not able to continue at break-neck speed long enough to complete my latest project. After a period of rest restored my energy, a new idea had taken root in my mind, and I abandoned the previous ones.

Now that I have the desire and endurance, I will complete this project. A more reasonable work pace will help. Once my forty days of journaling are completed, I will re-examine activities I have put aside. Maybe I was not ready to address them for some deeper spiritual reason. On the other hand, perhaps my priorities have changed. With abundant physical stamina and divine passion, I will pursue one task at a time as I am inspired and guided. Desire will lead to intention so I can follow through to each task's completion.

Now that I am over sixty, I wonder if my energy will begin to fade. Will I still be able to get up and dance with abandon when I am ten or twenty years older? I have watched loved ones slow down as they grow older. I have seen how they let go of things that have previously been an important part of their lives. My mother-in-law loved to bake, and family members and friends begged for her cookie recipes. Fortunately, she shared them without eliminating an essential ingredient, as her mother-in-law was known to do. When she passed away at 95, her baking days were long over, but she lived alone, drove a car, looked fantastic, and remained a sweet, loving soul until her final moments.

I greatly admired my mother-in-law because she graciously accepted the changes in her life. She adapted to her diminishing energy and honored her own needs. In the past, we affectionately called her a "martyr" because she did not want to bother anyone. During her last few years, she allowed others to cook for her and help with tasks around the home. Will I be as accepting when I can no longer do as much? I hope I will be able to adapt as well when I get older.

Balance implies stability, not just in our bodies, but also in our entire being. We are constantly in a state of flux and must make frequent shifts to maintain dynamic equilibrium. Our cells immediately sense when we are physically compromised and fly into action. They release hormones and work a little harder to restore homeostasis.

Balance is also related to authenticity. When we are authentic, we honor our true nature to maintain harmony within. When we are out of balance, stress occurs and can lead to anxiety and illness. To maintain emotional health and wellness, we need to keep our actions in alignment with our thoughts, feelings, and beliefs.

Balance is also critical with relationships. While boundaries are needed so others do not take advantage, we need to generously share our gifts and fulfill our earthly obligations. We need to learn how to serve others without depleting ourselves. Challenges will arise in marriages, friendships, and partnerships. Differences in personality can create havoc and inequality if a domineering person takes advantage of the submissive member of the duo.

At the intuitive level, we find balance through centering. Yogis and senseis encourage us to move and breathe from our center, from a state of wholeness. Along the midline of the body below the navel and nestled in front of the spine is a point known as the *Hara* or *tan tien*. Our soul's power or the center of our being is believed to stem from this location.

This teaching parallels what I learned from the *Blueprint for the Human Spirit*, my "inner guru." Hidden deep within our core is the key to equilibrium. As spiritual beings, we learn to tap into this sacred source to achieve stability and fulfill commitments. This is where the will resides and empowers us to remain true to our nature and purpose. When we trust our inner knowing and follow its perfect guidance, we can avoid the conflict of going in multiple directions at once. Instead of being tempted to abandon our current project, we can acknowledge new ideas, then document and file them under "Bright Ideas" for future consideration. Then, we can let them go so we remain centered and on course.

Ego enjoys putting us in our place. It keeps us humble by knocking us off our spiritual pedestal. When we temporarily lose our footing, we can simply breathe and pray ourselves back on track. Solid and secure in the Presence, we can return to a state of balance and remain true to who we are and why we are here. Balance becomes effortless when we are in alignment with truth.

I am grateful for the insights I have received about balance from the *Blueprint* and other spiritual masters and continue to integrate these teachings into my way of being. As Essence, I know that we do not need to struggle to achieve or maintain balance. It is now easier for me to maintain homeostasis and restore equilibrium if I fall off center. Instead of running incessantly on the treadmill of doing and expending more energy than necessary, I am learning to *be*. Instead of being pulled in multiple directions at once, I allow what is.

As I bear my soul and dive deeper beneath the surface with each confession, I discover more about myself. I am exposing hidden issues and blocks I thought I had released years ago. I am also uncovering more profound truths from the *Blueprint*. What a blessing! I cannot wait to see what is revealed tomorrow. Today I am the picture of balance, authenticity, and centeredness. When I make a lousy shot on the golf course, I will breathe, smile, and let it go. The next one will be better.

Affirmation:

I keep my thoughts, feelings, and actions balanced in alignment to fully express the truth of my being.

DAY 10

From Resentful to Grateful

You turned my wailing into dancing; you removed my sackcloth and clothed me with joy.
– Psalm 30:11

CONFESSION:

I am grateful, but I feel guilty for a life filled with abundant blessings.

No matter how hard you work to get ahead or how much you have to give up getting ahead, people are jealous. They only see what you have, not the challenges you overcame. To excel in my career, I worked long and hard to complete projects. I had little or no social life. To be successful, I moved at least once a year, leaving family and friends behind, venturing alone into unfamiliar cities.

Do not get me wrong because I am grateful for every career opportunity. Each one taught me something useful and prepared me for this moment. However, each choice came with a trade-off. I had to let go of something I valued to take the next step up the ladder. I gave up the comforts of home to travel for my job. The chance to visit spectacular sites around the country made this worthwhile. I left the stability of a relationship for a promotion and spent many lonely nights questioning this decision. However, I knew I would grow to resent anyone who held me back. At that time, my career was more important.

Some claim success comes from pure luck. Not true. Thomas Edison was right when he said, "The harder you work, the luckier you get." A relative once made a comment that I was just lucky to have married a successful man. I reminded this loved one that long before I met my husband, I put myself through college and graduate school, and I worked diligently for many years.

No doubt, this individual forgot that while I was gainfully employed, I supported many members of my family. I wondered if I reacted negatively to this comment because of underlying guilt or feelings of unworthiness. I am grateful for abundance and for a loving, supportive spouse. However, I wish other family members did not have to struggle to make ends meet. At the same time, I believe we create our own destiny. I made different life choices.

I have far more to be thankful for than a comfortable lifestyle. I am also grateful for my talents—creativity, writing ability, computer skills, and program planning expertise—and have worked extremely hard to develop them. As a teen, I felt inept. I was shy, introverted, and too fearful to try new things. To make matters worse, my older sister was extremely creative and outgoing. I was a year behind her in school and hid in her shadow, envious of her talents and knack for attracting boys. Years later, she admitted that she was jealous of my scholastic abilities.

It was not until I went to college and was on my own that I blossomed. I discovered I could accomplish anything I decided to do. I let my creativity out to play and became confident in social settings. Surprisingly, these changes occurred while attending a strict Bible college for a year—the most challenging time of my life. I was perceived as being too worldly, blamed for things I did not do, and restricted to the campus for not following unreasonable rules. I had made the proverbial jump from the frying pan of a conservative home life into the fire of an even more fundamental and judgmental educational institution.

While fraught with negativity, that year of religious torment is responsible for many positive changes in my life. A job opportunity led me to transfer to a different college and pursue a fulfilling career in nursing. In addition, the religious beliefs and standards were so extreme, I realized they were not for me. I walked away from this uncompromising version of Christianity and never looked back. Most importantly, I learned to stand up for myself. It took years to let go of the anger and finally embrace the blessing from this experience, but now I am grateful. Still, I would love to see the disapproving eye rolls of my former professors if they knew what I believe and teach today!

While many folks seem entitled and resent those with means, others are jumping on the gratitude bandwagon. The movement includes radio stations, spiritual practices, prayers and affirmations, special operations for troops, social networks, recipes, songs, poetry, festivals, and essential oils. There are even cafes and a brewery by this name—Generosity. Colgate University provides gratitude stoles for graduates to give to the special person who helped them the most in achieving their educational goals. And let us not forget Thanksgiving, our special holiday that brings this loving energy to the forefront.

The University of California at Berkeley is also committed to expanding the science of gratitude with an entire course of study. Through research, they discovered that those who practice gratitude have stronger immune systems and lower blood pressure, more positive emotions, and higher levels of joy, optimism, and happiness. They are more generous and compassionate, and they feel less lonely and isolated.

Our cells must jump for joy when we express appreciation. Gratitude does far more than help us to be healthy. It is the gateway to knowing and experiencing the presence of God. Years ago, as I struggled to meditate, a friend suggested starting with gratitude. What a gift! Now when I pause in silence and focus on that for which I am most thankful, I immediately feel the Presence of God within and around me. My body tingles and tears come to my eyes. In this state of Oneness, I am inspired and open to receive guidance for the day. I also begin healings with a prayer of intention and gratitude for what we will receive. I know that with God and gratitude, all things are good and possible.

I am most grateful for the *Blueprint*. This amazing metaphysical and mystical guide for conscious, compassionate living transformed me and brought meaning to my life. At the same time, it has increased my guilt. When I am not writing about it or do not have a calendar full of speaking engagements, I feel guilty. My dream is to share the *Blueprint's* sacred teaching and uplift humanity with its universal wisdom. I can never give back enough to compensate for the many benefits I received from this amazing gift, but I will try. In the past, I diluted my focus by getting involved with many non-profit organizations. Now that I have renewed my commitment to the *Blueprint*, I will do my best every day to stay the course. For this amazing opportunity and for how it continues to guide my unfolding, I am eternally grateful.

I would be remiss if I did not express my gratitude for the remarkable women in my life. They generously support me, believe in my efforts, and offer guidance. My spiritual sisters are one of my greatest blessings. When we sit in a sacred circle, share our insights, and affirm our intentions, something magical happens. We sense the true meaning of synergy and experience firsthand that, "where two or three are gathered," God's presence is known, and miracles happen. I also appreciate their honesty and their willingness to remind me if I wander from the straight and narrow.

When we pause to count our blessings, we open ourselves to receive even more. Gratitude ignites the movement of grace and allows loving energy to flow to, through, and as us. As beloved children of God, we deserve every gift of grace. For each one, I am grateful.

.

Affirmation:

I graciously receive everything the Universe provides and live in a state of gratitude for abundant wisdom, peace, love, and joy.

DAY 11

From Expectations to Acceptance

Those who were seen dancing were thought to be insane by those who could not hear the music.
– Friedrich Nietzsche

CONFESSION:

Instead of accepting what is, I am quick to judge and have high expectations for others and myself.

Spiritual masters teach us to accept and allow what is, but I still struggle to let go of judgment. I truly wish to reach the state where I know all is well before my mouth reveals my true feelings and blurts aloud, "What *were* they thinking?" I know expectations only set us up to fail. When we have expectations of others, they also fail in our eyes.

I blame my tendency to believe I am right and judge because of my strict childhood. How strict was it, you ask? We affectionately nicknamed my mother "Proper Patty." She wanted us—and everything we said and did—to measure up to church standards. She wanted us to look the part because appearances were the first clue if we were slacking. To this day, her typical response is to "Tsk, Tsk, Tsk" in disapproval, just like her own mother. She "tsked" so much our parakeet even mimicked her!

On one hand, I am glad she constantly reminded us to stand up straight and hold our heads up high. My siblings and I have her to thank for excellent posture. Kids today slouch and walk with their pelvis forward. Not very attractive! Oops, I cannot seem to break the habit to judge!

My sisters helped me correct my tendency to be pigeon-toed. They seemed to enjoy reminding me to straighten my feet. Today I still swing my right foot inward but usually place my feet straight ahead unless I am tired or uncomfortable. My sisters also reminded me to hold in my tummy. "Muffin tops" were not acceptable when we were young. As the years and pounds added up, I lost the battle of the bulge. Now I am working hard to get and stay in shape but am afraid my stomach will never be flat again.

When I was in the ninth grade, a boy in my class told me I had a receding chin and demonstrated what my profile looked like. I was devastated and felt ugly for the first time in my life. To this day, I unconsciously drop and extend my jaw to correct this flaw. I cannot believe how susceptible we are to criticisms and how they can affect our beliefs and behaviors. This same boy also made fun of my shapely lower extremities and nicknamed me "Banana Legs." A few years later, when he wanted to date me with my receding chin and curvy legs, I was not interested.

Now that I am quickly descending the backside of the proverbial hill, my appearance is becoming an issue. I would like to retain my youthful looks, but brown spots are taking up residence on my face and no amount of makeup will hide them. The skin on my neck has started to sag which further augments my lovely receding chin. Fine lines along my mouth are turning into deep gullies as I lose weight. I do not want to look like my grandmother in twenty years; her face was like a roadmap. I watch the changes with dismay but am determined to age gracefully. I hope a magic product that can turn back the clock will hit the market soon, but I am sure my expectations will prove disappointing. No matter what, I will not consider a facelift. I will just take off my reading glasses to blur my vision so I can only focus on my inner radiance.

When I notice something "wrong," immediately Miss Fix-It steps up to make it all better. Along with the tendency to criticize, I also blame this habit on a judgmental upbringing. For years, I tried to make everything okay and solve problems my family members faced. I immediately went into action and did everything possible to mend what was broken. It took years, but now I realize they may only have been venting and did not want interference. No doubt, I will need many more years of practice to stop reacting and going into fix-it mode.

We usually need to learn from our own mistakes. This could not be more evident than with my friend's experience with her children. Four of her five children had children without being married. She thought her boys would learn from their sister's experience a few years earlier, but NO! My friend screamed at her daughter for a month when she got pregnant at seventeen. When her youngest son got his girlfriend pregnant, she screamed for a week. When her two other sons continued the family tradition, she threw up her hands and said, "So what's new?" Obviously, she had to let go of her anger and expectations to welcome her new grandbabies with open arms. Fortunately, her boys are stepping up to the daddy-plate between softball games and are learning the hard way to be responsible single parents.

Although I have my own opinions about what is good and bad, or right and wrong, I believe everything happens for the highest good. I also believe that our meddling only makes things worse. Since everything is in perfect Divine Order, I intend to allow and not be so quick to judge. Matthew 7:1-3 tells us:

> *"Do not judge, or you too will be judged. For in the same way you judge others, you will be judged, and with the measure you use, it will*

be measured to you. Why do you look at the speck of sawdust in your brother's eye and pay no attention to the plank in your own eye?"

I do not need, or want, the added stress from striving to achieve my own unrealistic expectations. Instead, I forgive myself. I will also continue to remove the planks from my own eyes through this soul-cleansing exercise so I can look beyond appearances. I wish to see only Essence in others and myself. Since change is a process and requires practice, practice, practice, I will endeavor to keep working at this and not be too critical of myself when I slip. What is, is!

AFFIRMATION:

I release expectations and judgment to embrace what is. I know all is well and in perfect Divine Order.

Day 12

From Close-Minded to Openness

Any kind of dancing is better than no dancing at all.
– Lynda Barr

Confession:

I am not always open, ready, and willing to receive feedback or to consider different points of view.

Recently I had lunch with two spiritual sisters. We shared revelations and enjoyed each other's company. One is a new friend, so I was extremely interested in learning more about her life, family, and spiritual journey. She mirrored a trait of mine that I know requires some work. I often butt in when others are talking, eager to describe a similar experience. Instead of actively listening, I am more interested in sharing my own story.

This delightful lady shared insight that I should "preach." I have heard this before in healings, but do not like this word because it brings up negative images of red-faced ministers pointing their fingers at me and condemning me for every sin I did or did not commit. The guilt and shame I felt was intense. While the scars still mar my soul, they have not stopped me from becoming a spiritual teacher. I am more than willing to share what I have learned from the *Blueprint for the Human Spirit.* I also look forward to a time when I will regularly have speaking engagements on my calendar. I am eager to share the profound life-changing experiences the *Blueprint* has inspired.

Unlike me, my husband's family is more closed-lipped. They keep personal matters to themselves and often from each other. They have a tendency to "protect" other family members from bad news. Eventually, the word gets out. Family members get upset, and feelings are hurt anyway.

I used to be overly sensitive to feedback and criticism. When I first joined a writing group, I wanted them to like what I shared and to compliment my content and style. I was not as open to constructive ideas as I am today. My little ego was more fragile then. This group designed a special process for giving feedback that could benefit all our relationships. We began with "I really liked…" Then we made a suggestion without criticism; "Have you considered…?" This approach was easier to swallow.

I was also sensitive about the *Blueprint.* As a member of a MasterMind group, I often shared insights, ideas, and intentions I received. This was my creation, my baby, my gift to the world, and I did not appreciate negative comments. When a member of my group said she was tired of hearing about it, I was devastated. How could my friend, someone who was like a spiritual mother to me, think and say that? My entire life, as well as my spiritual evolution was based on this model!

After the incident I searched my heart and realized how attached I was to "my work." Slowly I began to see it fade away. The cells within the Matrix started to merge into one amorphous whole. I no longer needed its conceptual framework to guide my every thought, word, and deed. Since I did not want to be addicted to or limited by anything, I knew I needed to be willing to release all attachments in my life. This included the *Blueprint.* I may not have had to let it go, but I had to be willing.

Eventually I changed my perspective. It is no longer "my *Blueprint,*" but a sacred teaching from the Universe. I am the vessel through which it was born and am free to learn from it and share it. However, I do not own it. I may still be compelled to bring it to light, but I know if I do not, that is okay too.

Of my three sisters, I am closest to the oldest. We were born sixteen months apart and are soul twins, but opposites. She has dark hair, and I was born blonde; her eyes are brown, mine are blue; she was more creative, carefree, and outgoing as a teen while I was quiet, introverted, and studious. When I was in a work mode, she focused on spiritual studies and *vice versa*. We are so close we know when something is going on with the other and go out of our way to get in touch. I can say anything to her and her to me, without taking offense.

Once my sister called upset about an upcoming vacation. Her stepdaughter invited her and her husband to go with their family for a week to the outer banks of North Carolina. She was looking forward to the trip until she learned they had also invited two of her grandsons' friends. She felt this was no longer a family vacation and wanted to stay home and avoid the chaos the youngsters would create.

I suggested she view this trip from a different perspective. Her son-in-law recently had a heart attack and needed a rest. Her husband was looking forward to fishing in the ocean. Her stepdaughter was overwhelmed with a new job and needed a change of scenery. I suggested my sister embrace the trip, not for herself, but as something to do for the family. Immediately, she got the message and changed her point of view. She called a few times from the shore enthralled with its beauty and the peace she felt there. The boys entertained themselves and the two friends were an unexpected blessing. This trip was exactly what she needed and became the highlight of her summer.

I was reminded of how important shifts in perception are when my husband, a gifted photographer, prepared for two classes he was presenting for the new photo club in our community. He shared his outline, and after reviewing it, I encouraged him to create a PowerPoint slide show to illustrate what he intended to say. Since his talks were about one of the visual arts, I was quite adamant that he needed visuals to enhance his presentation. He was resistant at first, but I shared my experiences in using slides to highlight the salient points of a presentation to keep myself on track. Since he lacked any experience with PowerPoint, he hesitated to try it.

In a few minutes, I drafted a few slides using some of his photos. Then I emailed a link to a YouTube video that demonstrated the basics. Once he overcame his initial fear, he became bolder and more creative. Now he is hooked. He is excited and focused on this project. I believe he also understands how I become so engaged in my own projects and how exciting it is to create something unique.

When we open our hearts and minds, we step boldly into the future. We look beyond what has always been and embrace the possibilities. We welcome the opportunity to accept what we were born to be. Instead of feeling limited, we boldly expand our awareness and develop skills so we can more fully express our divinity through our humanity. Then, we can share our love and our gifts more eloquently and brilliantly with the world.

AFFIRMATION:

I am open, willing, and ready for everything life has to offer, and I embrace every opportunity to learn from serving others.

Day 13

From Desire to Contentment

Then young women will dance and be glad, young men and old as well. I will turn their mourning into gladness: I will give them comfort and joy instead of sorrow.
– Jeremiah 31:13

Confession:

I am not content with what I know and have an insatiable desire to discover more about God and myself.

I am a spiritual junkie. I yearn for revelations and awareness as much as I crave chocolate. For years, I could not get enough supernatural sugar. I attended every seminar I could, read every book recommended by fellow students of the transcendent, and sought guidance from every psychic within a fifty-mile radius. I studied the teachings of the Masters. Like a thirsty sponge, I drank it all in. I could not get enough. I sampled every spiritual practice known to humankind from ancient rituals to new age techniques.

Eventually, I let them go. They were not right for me. I realized many so-called "spiritual teachers" had huge egos, seemed phony, and their techniques did not produce the results I desired. Instead of encouraging me to seek guidance from within, they created dependency on their input—for a price, of course.

The first time I realized it was possible to receive inner guidance was during a visioning experience at the Center for Creative Leadership. Using guided imagery, the facilitator took us on a mental journey where we met a previously selected individual and asked a question we had written before the exercise. I asked my older sister, the person who introduced me to spirituality, what I should do next. I had recently quit my job and had no idea what career path to take. The guidance was simple—the answers are within you.

Before I finally took this insight to heart, I became a devoted seeker, and I spent many years and countless registration and consultant fees on the quest for greater awareness. The more I searched, the more disappointed I became. I longed for something more, something unknown. I continued a life of "if only's"—if only I had a better job and a higher salary; if only I had a newer, better car; if I only had another degree; if I only had the perfect partner; if only chocolate did not have calories… Now my "if only" was about finding the right spiritual teacher and practices.

On my spiritual quest, I traveled to many sacred sites. I laid down in an ancient medicine wheel in Sedona, walked the labyrinth at the ruins of a monastery in Central America, circled Stonehenge, knelt at the graves of saints in Rome, and followed the path of the Zen masters in Japan. I tried to feel energy from those who blazed spiritual trails before me, only to be disappointed. The more I searched, the further I needed to go to find God. The metaphysical maze I explored only led to dead ends. I wanted to discover more, but where should I look?

After reading *The Secret* by Rhonda Byrne, I became quite adept in metaphysical manifestation. I envisioned and affirmed tangible things and watched them appear. I finally realized material goods did not nourish my soul, but only fed my craving ego. I had yet to discover that all we truly need is to know ourselves and Oneness with God. Only then would the suffering of separation dissolve and the longing disappear.

Some fellow travelers raved about the benefits they received from studying with their guru, so I decided I also needed one. As I passionately affirmed that a spiritual teacher would come into my life, a voice spoke to me. "*What am I? Chopped liver?"* I obviously had the perfect inner teacher, but I did not recognize it as a higher authority and failed to embrace its divine guidance. At the time, I did not realize all the insights I needed were coming directly into my awareness and were evolving into the *Blueprint for the Human Spirit.*

For years, I continued to read and study, perhaps out of habit, until the Universe intervened. My husband faced a series of health issues that demanded my full-time attention. Therefore, I backed out of book groups and attended church less frequently. I no longer felt compelled to go to workshops or seek guidance from intuitive healers. This pause from my incessant quest allowed truth to sink in.

After a long and arduous journey, my search finally led me within to a place of meaningful silence where I no longer needed others to tell me what to believe and how to practice. I stopped looking out there and began trusting my inner knowings. I became a seer, one filled with an inner peace that quenched my thirst. I now realize my longing forced me to snatch scraps from the table of others instead of enjoying the feast within. As Rumi, the 13th century Sufi mystic said, "I have been a seeker and still am, but I stopped asking the books and the stars. I started listening to the teachings of my soul."

On our amazing journey, the Universe spoon-feeds us one morsel of truth at a time when we are ready to digest it. We crave more, but eventually discover deeper realities. This becomes exceedingly clear when working with clients. When asked if a soul mate and happiness are in their future, I know they truly desire unconditional love, and only Oneness with God will bring satisfaction. Inquiries about a new job or promotion reveal all they need is to show up every day as the Presence of God and share the Love that they are. The specifics of what they do, who they serve, or where they work are not important.

When we are ready for deeper truths, they will be revealed. I recently heard a minister explain the meaning of hell. He said it is not just a burning garbage pit outside an ancient city or the horrific place preachers use to keep us on the straight and narrow. Hell represents purification. Fire and heat symbolically eliminate negative thoughts and beliefs that separate us from the Divine. That is exactly what this forty-day period of confessing is all about—a purification process. I am letting all the garbage, all the residual blocks and fears come to the surface. As I look at my life with new eyes, my experiences are transmuted into something holy. This is alchemy, the nature of the quest and the growth process. As we become more aware, suffering is transformed into joy. We shift the false perception of separation and duality so we can recognize and embrace Oneness. We release desires and realize that everything we want is already within our grasp.

I recently took Mother to St. Augustine and while we waited for the tram, I read the promotional flyer. It included a list of special discounts available to us. With the possibility of saving a few dollars, I read them aloud to Mother. "A free soft drink at a deli; ¼ lb. of fudge if you bought a pound; a free charm; 10% discount on body candy…" Mother immediately asked what body candy was. After I composed myself and gave her a watered-down explanation, she replied that she could not imagine anyone wanting *that.* Then she said, "I'd rather have fudge!" Me too! We nearly fell off the bench laughing.

I have finally quit seeking, and I no longer consume saccharine-coated advice from so-called prophets. I have discovered the one and only true source. Truth flows direct from within and dwells in the core of my being. I already have a guru—the *Blueprint for the Human Spirit.* I listen and learn from its infinite wisdom and am so grateful

AFFIRMATION:

I release my addiction to seeking and embrace the truth of my being. I am and have all that I desire—Oneness with God.

DAY 14

From Controlling to Allowing

If you've got nothing to dance about, find a reason to sing.
– Melody Carstairs

CONFESSION:

I do not like being a worker bee where others tell me what to do and how to do it; I would rather lead a project.

I take charge. When a crisis arises, I am the first to jump up and fix the problem. This may be a result of my nursing background and training, or it may be my inherent caregiving nature. Regardless, I just can't stop myself when faced with a challenge.

Here is an example. In the middle of a vintage fashion show held by the women's group at our church, a woman passed out. I was on the platform narrating the occasion. When no one in the audience of 450 responded to my request for a doctor, I sprang into action and ran down the aisle. I instructed those nearby to move chairs aside and place the woman on the floor. Then, I asked someone to call 911 and began CPR with one of the models for fashion show who happened to be a cardiac nurse.

By the time the paramedics arrived, the lady seemed fine. She did not want to go to the hospital and miss the rest of the event. Fortunately, we insisted, and it is a good thing because she had a heart attack. After the paramedics rolled her away, I took a deep breath, returned to the podium, and continued the show. I prefer to avoid life and death situations like this, but when the need arises, I am ready, willing, and able.

A year and a half before my father died, Mother fell and broke her hip. She had been dad's primary caregiver for nearly twenty years after he was paralyzed on the left side from a stroke. During this critical time, she could no longer care for Dad, so the entire family stepped up to help. While assisting, I discovered my folks also needed help with legal and insurance affairs, and repairs and organization. Their home was filled with items that needed to be sorted, eliminated, or stored. My sisters nominated me to be the "bad guy" and crack the whip. I stepped up, worked with my parent's attorney and insurance companies, scheduled repairs, organized the cleanup, and brought everything up to date. Mother now calls me "Sarge."

On one hand, my folks appreciated the help, but Mother was uncomfortable with the speed of my efforts and my tendency to push everyone to complete the project. She particularly resented cleaning out her desk and files, insisting we made her "throw away her entire life." Instead, we honored her life by giving her the opportunity to relive it. She found letters from friends who had passed and sent them on to their children. She told funny stories about us kids and surprised us with cards, letters, and papers that she had kept for years.

I do not mind overseeing project teams, but I do not like being told what to do or how to do it. When that happens, the Defiant One shows up and stomps her feet. Perhaps I resist authority because I was not permitted to stand up for myself as a child. Because I am blessed with the gift of organization, I am usually the one telling others what to do. I keep team members well informed and communicate expectations on who is to do what by when. I proficiently facilitate the process, so the job is completed on time and to the best of our collective ability. I also admit that I am impatient with those who are inefficient and ineffective.

Day 14

In years past, my management style has been equated with a Bulldozer. As president of my alumni association, I brought the organization's activities up to date. To do this, I had to bypass a staff member who blocked our progress. When meeting minutes and follow-up plans were not distributed, I went directly to support staff for assistance. I overstepped my bounds as a volunteer and earned the nickname "The Empress." The names I used to describe the ineffective employee were less flattering. A few years later as I moved forward on my spiritual path, I recognized the error of my ways and my part in the conflict. I attempted unsuccessfully to locate this individual to apologize.

Since then, my approach has softened. I still get the job done, but I do it with more heart. I also avoid taking on leadership roles for other organizations. I have learned the hard way that I cannot do everything for everyone and do it well all the time. I have learned to be more selective. However, I continue to facilitate the women's group at our church because I created the concept and launched this activity. It is my baby, and I will do my best to keep it going until it is time to turn it over.

The ability to delegate is critical for leaders and managers, whether the job is in the home, workplace, or community. While it may be easier or more expeditious to do the jobs ourselves, it is always preferable to share responsibility. During my first marriage, I did all the housework, laundry, cooking, cleaning, and paperwork without asking for help. I learned my lesson, and the second time around, I made sure this did not happen. When my husband proposed, I asked what he expected of a wife. Since I was working full-time, I let him know I did not intend to clean, vacuum, or wash windows. When he promised not to cancel his cleaning service, I gladly said "Yes." We have been together over thirty years, and to this day, I rarely clean.

I have also learned how to ask for help. For years, I expected my family to read my mind, anticipate my needs, and step up to the plate before I had to ask. This approach was not effective as they are not intuitive. Nor were they trained to have the high standards that were instilled in me by my mother!

Now, I use a little humor and say, "I will LET you set the table" or "I'll LET you do the dishes." They usually laugh and comply without complaining. I still wish I did not need to ask, but I am realistic.

When I was ill last winter, I felt completely out of control. I hardly had enough energy to take care of myself, let alone fulfill my responsibilities in the home. I was dependent on my husband for shopping, preparing meals, running errands, etc. If I wanted something, it was on his time and performed his way. I could not orchestrate the details, so I had to sit back and be a gracious receiver. Now I have greater empathy for those who are dependent. They have little influence over what happens to them and are at the mercy of their caregivers. No wonder my father was so frustrated when he could no longer use his hands creatively. I cannot imagine what I would do or how I would respond if I were no longer able to write and share the *Blueprint*.

Control is an illusion. We can do little to govern the circumstances around us. While Ego demands to be in charge, correct, obeyed, respected, and successful, Essence accepts and allows what is. The *Blueprint* revealed to me that when we surrender and let go of what the personality prefers, we can fully embrace and express the truth of our being. We can realize our highest potential and do it easily and effortlessly. We no longer need to struggle or strive, but have the power, ability, and freedom to express all that we are—beloved expressions of God.

Since everything is in perfect Divine Order, we should just leave well-enough alone and go with the flow. This is not easy for a take-charge person, but I continue to give it my best shot. At the same time, I encourage those around me not to expect miracles because personality transplants have not yet been created!

Affirmation:

I let go of control and allow what is so I can embrace and express Essence.

Day 15

From Oblivious to Aware

Life is a dance. Mindfulness is witnessing that dance.
– Amit Ray

Confession:

I have a hard head, so it usually takes a few cosmic whacks before I learn my lessons and become more aware.

I am a life-long student. I have completed nearly twenty years of formal education to obtain a nursing degree, Master's in Public Health, and a Doctorate in Holistic Health Sciences. I have read stacks of textbooks and memorized laundry lists of facts to pass tests, only to use a small portion of the knowledge. No doubt, I have forgotten more than I remember! Hours of cramming also resulted in little, if any, significant changes in my behavior. It almost seems a waste of time and effort.

Two coworkers did share their wisdom about how we adopt new health habits. First, we become aware of a health issue and realize there is something we can do about it. After hearing or seeing the same information a few times, it begins to sink in, and we are compelled to discover possible solutions. If this seems reasonable and doable, we test out the new behavior. Assuming we have a positive experience, we may repeat it until it eventually becomes a lifestyle change that helps us remain healthy and ward off illness. The most important part of this behavioral change process is the experiential component. If we do not try it on for size, we will never learn. We will never grow and change.

This process applies to all aspects of life. The Universe is obviously conspiring with our Higher Self in this learning process. If we fail to "get" something the first time, we receive one coincidental nudge after another. Ignoring these hints is impossible because if this gentle approach does not do the trick, we receive a cosmic whack that we cannot overlook or forget.

Long before I began my spiritual journey, I was a "tree hugger" and have actual photos of me hugging a tree to prove it. I was secretary of my high school's Earth Day activities the first year it was launched. Life was simpler in the country and in that era. We were self-sufficient and lived off the land. Conservation was not something we were concerned about until we experienced our first gas crisis.

Years later, while I was studying for my Master of Public Health, I became more aware of the need to recycle, reuse, and reduce to sustain our limited natural resources. I shared what I learned with my folks and made a couple of suggestions on how they could protect their trees, compost, and safeguard their land. Dad said he owned the property, and it was his to use as he pleased. He quoted the Bible verse from Genesis, which says man was given dominion over the earth. His literal interpretation was in keeping with that of the fundamental church they attended. I backed off, knowing my ideas were not welcomed.

Thanks to my metaphysical studies, I have a deeper, different understanding of the word "dominion." As conscious beings, we alone can consider the future and understand the potential effects of our actions. Because of this, we are responsible for sustaining Earth. The American Indians were masters at this. Before making a decision, they looked seven generations into the future to determine its impact. If we were that conscientious, we would not be facing an ecological crisis today.

Over time I finally got the message and my lessons about intuition were more explicit. As I began tapping into this inner guidance, I literally experienced a whack on the head. The cable on our daughter's garage door snapped and one side of the door fell on top of our SUV. As we tried to lift the door enough to get the vehicle out, a voice said to move. I did not immediately react, the second cable snapped, and the door came down on us. Fortunately, we were not injured. Because of this experience, however, I learned to pay more attention to that inner voice. Now, if I hear myself talking aloud, posing a mental question, or carrying on an inner dialogue, I listen and follow my intuition. The guidance is always right.

A lesson about loss was one of the most difficult and timely ones I have encountered. I spoke for a local spiritual group one Sunday and shared insights from the "Circle of Life," one of the *Blueprint's* sacred concepts. I described how we mature and how our obligations change. The talk included how we are responsible for ourselves, our children and dependents, and our earthly home. I also discussed my views on how life is eternal and how we are always connected with those who have transitioned.

After concluding my lesson, I returned home and received a call that my twenty-one-year-old niece had died in a car accident. This unexpected blow gave me an entirely different perspective on the "Circle of Life." Since I was repeating my talk one week later at another church, I added photos of my niece to my PowerPoint presentation. Her story deeply touched the congregation. Only by the grace of God was I able to maintain my composure while on the platform. Instead of giving lip service to the impact of loss and our eternal connections, I can now empathize with those suffering through the grief process. Tears still come to my eyes when I think of her. Sometimes life's lessons hurt for an exceedingly long time.

As the *Blueprint* evolved into a beautiful matrix and disclosed its sacred truths, I learned—one revelation at a time. I discovered who I am, why I am here, and how we are one with God. This holistic model became the framework through which I view life. However, it was not until I experienced it firsthand that it really sank in.

Early one morning in 2001, I sat on my lanai and quickly went into a meditative state. During the next hour and a half, I experienced a dramatic episode in the lives of fifteen different people. Their lives and the scenes were so vivid I thought they were past lives. Now I know they are archetypes. Each one revealed a shift in consciousness that was critical for my soul growth and transformation.

For example, I encountered an American Indian shaman from nearly 1,000 years ago. He had great reverence for the earth and insight into the impact of everyone on the environment. He used his special gifts to heal his people and encouraged them to live in harmony with nature. I resonated with this individual because I sense a deep connection with indigenous cultures and have a strong commitment to ecology.

This experience was by far the most powerful and life-altering I have ever had. From this moment on, the *Blueprint* was no longer just an interesting intellectual exercise. It came to life and became part of me. I deeply felt what these individuals experienced because their stories paralleled my own. Only then was I able to fully understand and integrate the *Blueprint's* teachings into my way of being. I am still gleaning deeper truths and wisdom from these amazing archetypes and plan to share them so others can also benefit from their amazing stories.

AFFIRMATION:

I embrace every encounter and experience, knowing each is an opportunity to learn and expand my awareness.

DAY 16

From Guilty to Blameless

We should consider every day lost on which we have not danced at least once.
– Friedrich Nietzsche

CONFESSION:

I am a victim of religious abuse and suffered with extreme guilt and feelings of unworthiness for many years.

When I read Joan Borysenko's book, *Guilt is the Teacher, Love is the Lesson*, I sobbed uncontrollably. This was the first time I had heard about religious abuse and the impact of what had happened to me began to sink in. I was told repeatedly that I was unworthy and tainted by original sin. Since ministers supposedly spoke the truth, I had no choice but to believe them. What I heard is the exact opposite of the blessings that children receive at Unity churches: "You are loved, special, and important." I wonder what my life would have been like if I had heard those affirming words.

I was five years old and in first grade the first time I felt shame. I was the target of unwelcomed attention from a boy who was a couple of years older than me. One day while I was getting a drink of water at the fountain, this boy opened the restroom door, unzipped his pants, and exposed himself to me. I was mortified and called him a "devil," the worst word I knew at that time. He told me I was an angel. I never told a soul about this devastating experience because I felt guilty. I believed it was my fault.

On my spiritual journey, I have learned that religious teachings and rituals that diminish us and separate us from Source, God, Essence, or our Higher Self, are abusive. In addition, any spiritual guide that makes us dependent on them is leading us down a dead-end street. While studying the major religions of the world, I discovered that many of their core messages have been adulterated. Truths have been misinterpreted or twisted by church leaders for power, money, and ego gratification. One example is the mile-long list of "thou shall not's" that I was told to live by as a young girl. No doubt, stodgy old men compiled them!

There is one rule that I have yet to understand. Why was I not allowed to wear open-toed shoes, sling-backs, and sandals? Maybe you can enlighten me about what is so immoral about toe cleavage. I confess I have rejected this rule along with the no makeup, no jewelry, no short sleeves, no pants, no hair cutting, no shopping or working on Sunday, no TV, no nothing...

Another no-no from my rigid religious upbringing was dancing. I love to dance and do it every possible chance I get. When I watched *Footloose*, I swear they were demonstrating my life on the screen. Unlike these bold kids, however, I was not strong or confident enough to stand up to authority. My sisters may have snuck out to attend proms, but I was too afraid I would be caught. In addition, I was a geek, so no one asked me to go.

Alcohol was also prohibited. This rule I understand as it lowers your level of consciousness, so I imbibe sparingly. The Bible includes a story of how Jesus performed a miracle at a wedding and turned water into wine. When we asked our parents why it was okay for them to drink wine, we were told it was not wine but grape juice, and we should not take this literally. If wine was not actually wine, is it possible that a day of creation is longer than twenty-four hours? When we inquired about inconsistencies, we were told it was a sin to question the scriptures. Obviously, independent thinking was discouraged, and deeper truths remained hidden.

We were also permitted only to read the King James Version of the Bible as it was believed this text came straight from the mouth of God. Obviously, the church leaders who made this decision were not aware of the "evolution" of the Bible, other translations, and the lost gospels. Other sacred teachings were also rejected and believed to be misguided. This narrow stance severely limited my grasp of spirituality. In fact, for many years I did not know the difference between religion and spirituality.

It pains me to see religious conflicts around the world. Why not just let everyone believe and worship as he or she wishes—if no one is harmed in the process? I hold the opinion that there are as many paths to God as there are people. For this reason, I do not support evangelism with its intention to convert people to the "one true faith." When taken to the extreme, this leads to genocide.

You might wonder if by sharing teachings from the *Blueprint* I am attempting to convert others to my way of thinking. Not so! In fact, the *Blueprint* contains universal truths that I believe are relevant to all faiths. However, I only share it as an example of what can happen when we tap into our inner guidance and encourage everyone to discover their own path. I share the *Blueprint* as a framework for exploring our inner landscape.

My studies have revealed that the world's major religions hold the same core beliefs. We have a direct connection with a higher power, and we are one with each other and nature. Obviously, the 13th century Sufi mystic Rumi embraced this. He wrote a poem that encourages us to see beyond the illusion of duality and separation. "Out beyond right doing and wrongdoing there is a field. I will meet you there."

For this very reason, the former minister from our church, Jim Rosemergy, was inspired to write the *Creed of the Heart*. "Our God is love. Our race is human. Our religion is oneness." How perfect! No rules or laws, just love. With love, we can look beyond outward appearances and see only Essence. With eyes of love, we see that we are part of the whole. We are all the same—beloved children of God.

The God of my youth was a powerful ogre, a critical man with a long white beard and crinkled eyes who lived up in the sky and passed severe judgment on my every thought, word, and deed. I was guilty for just being born and scared to death of this tyrant. For some reason, if the minister ever told us that God was love, I did not hear it. I was so brainwashed by the negativity that oozed like soul slime from the pulpit, I shut down. When I went to college, I walked away and only went back to church years later to sing in a choir. As soon as the minister stepped onto the platform, my ears, mind, and heart closed as tight as a drum.

Only men are ministers in my parent's fundamentalist church. They embrace a literal translation of first Corinthians indicating that women are to be silent in church. They would not support my higher purpose, to share truths from the *Blueprint for the Human Spirit*, because I am a woman, and the content is not compatible with their interpretation of the Bible. I wonder what my grandfather, a forefather of my parent's church, would say at the very thought of his granddaughter "preaching." Instead of rolling over in his grave, I am sure he is rejoicing that I am free of guilt that previously blocked the full expression of Essence. For the opportunity to share the *Blueprint*, and for the insights I continue to receive, I am ecstatic and profoundly grateful. And I no longer feel guilty. I am free.

Affirmation:

I am free of guilt and live a life of love, peace, and joy, which reflects the Essence of my being.

Day 17

From Fearful to Peaceful

Daily dance uplifts the soul to spiritual realms.
– Lailah Gifty Akita

Confession:

I lived in fear of punishment for wrongdoing and still recoil at the threat of violence and terrorism.

September 11th was seared in our brains as we watched with horror as the Twin Towers came crumbling down. I was angry with those who took the lives of the innocent and joined the throngs who felt we must capture and punish those responsible for creating such havoc. This response automatically rises to the surface each year as we see the horrible images replayed on TV and relive the trauma. There was only one voice of reason in the news: Richard Geer, a Buddhist, encouraged us to take the high road, release our suffering, and not retaliate. He was harshly criticized.

Some faiths, like Unity and the Quakers, also promote peace and nonresistance. Although I subscribe to this way of thinking because it is compatible with the *Blueprint*, I was slow to get back on track after the terrorist attack. I learned to be fearful. God-fearing folk were praised in the church of my youth, and my parents fervently prayed their four daughters would marry God-fearing men.

With this negative belief system and the threat of eternal punishment, is it any wonder I felt vulnerable and was so frightened?

Desert Storm began before I started on my spiritual path. I was devastated, convinced that it marked the beginning of Armageddon and the end of time. I had just gotten married the second time and was happy and secure in a wonderful relationship. I was angry that my happiness would be short-lived, and my wonderful world would go up in smoke. Obviously, the messages from fear-spouting ministers were still burned into my brain.

I had no idea that my fears as a child were so obvious until I went to my fortieth high school reunion. One of my former classmates told me she was thrilled to see me so happy and free. She did not know that I had stepped out of my fearful, shy, and insecure box until I gave a hilarious performance of Patsy Cline's song, *She's Got You.* I never realized that I lived in fear. However, it was obvious to others. Fear was just a way of life. With acts of terrorism, it floods back to the surface.

Conflicts in the Middle East and throughout the world increased my concern for a niece when she was in the Army Reserves. I hoped and prayed that she was not called to active duty. After seeing the impact of the Viet Nam war on my ex and former brother-in-law, I know how horrible it is. Alcoholism, drug abuse, flashbacks, PTSD, physical wounds, and permanent disabilities affect our soldiers and their families. I look forward to a time of peace when we live in harmony and no longer feel the need to protect ourselves.

Because of my spiritual beliefs, I am a peacenik. I also believe military options are not viable solutions for the struggles in the world. Albert Einstein said, "No problem can be solved from the same level of consciousness that created it." In other words, retaliating with bullets and bombs will not stop terrorism. We cannot change minds, hearts, and beliefs with guns. What is the solution? How can we respond in a way that will make a positive difference?

Jesus told us to love our enemies. Abraham Lincoln said, "I destroy my enemies when I make them my *friends*." The Law of Mind Action reveals that "thoughts held in mind produce after their own kind." If this is true, we will not create peace in the world until we know inner peace.

To change the world, we need a critical mass to embrace an idea until it becomes self-sustaining. The story of the hundredth monkey illustrates how the behavior of primates on an island changed when just one more began washing its sweet potatoes before eating them. How many people will it take to reach a critical mass that can bring world peace? Only 1/10 of 1% of the population, less than 800,000—not that many, considering the world population is nearly 8 billion! If enough of us find inner tranquility, world peace can become a reality.

I recently watched a documentary about Bhutan, the happiest country in the world. Their Gross National Happiness quotient exceeds that of everywhere else on the planet. Everyone smiles, enjoys life, and lives in harmony. They have no conflict with neighboring nations and no issues with each other. Perhaps it is because they are the last isolated Buddhist country in the world. They have a stable ecosystem because tourism is limited. The fact they are one of the poorest countries does not limit the smiles that radiate from the residents. Obviously, greed, competition, and inept politicians do not taint their society. Bhutan's first democratic leader, a twenty-eight-year-old graduate of Wheaton College and Oxford, is effectively maintaining balance as his country opens its doors to the age of technology. We could learn a great deal from these enlightened people.

The *Blueprint* taught me about the nature of fear and why it exists. It stems from the universal perception of duality. We view ourselves as distinct physical beings and believe we are at risk of dying and losing all we hold dear. We also think that we are separate from Spirit/Source/Self and others. This false sense of self, the Ego, automatically responds with fear when it is threatened. It creates attachments to beliefs, addictions to things and the adoption of behaviors to fill the void.

This cycle continues until we experience a shift in awareness and embrace the truth of our being. In the physical realm, for example, fear of death, pain, and lack causes us to respond with greed, competition, and jealousy. We embrace money, possessions, power, and position to feel whole. Until we trust the Universe, each other, and ourselves to provide for all our needs, we will not transcend our fears and enjoy abundant health, wealth, and happiness. In truth, we are immortal, spiritual beings who never die. We are "godlings" and our spiritual nature is Love. When I finally realized that I am not just a body with a soul but a spiritual being enjoying a human experience, my fear of death disappeared.

When my sister performed a healing on me, I communicated with a cousin who had passed, and I told her I would see her soon. For three weeks, I thought I was going to die and was afraid. The *Blueprint* helped me release these fears and realize that while my body might cease to live, my Essence would never die. Energetically speaking, I know that we always were part of the whole and always will be. When we die, we may no longer inhabit this body, but we will return to Source. Once again, we will become part of the eternal Presence.

I am on a path of peace and know I am safe. Regardless of what happens in the world out there, I, as Essence, can never be hurt or killed, but will live forever. On this day, and every day, I will look into the eyes of those who cross my path and see only the truth of their being. I will not see terrorists or abusers, but I will see only the spark of the Divine within them. We are One, all beloved children of God. This is what unites us and makes us part of the whole. I am part of the critical mass that is committed to inner harmony. By knowing serenity within, we will give birth to world peace so everyone can enjoy a life filled with love, not fear.

AFFIRMATION:

As a spiritual being, I release all fear to enjoy peace within and harmony with all Creation.

DAY 18

From Prayer to Presence

In a society that worships love, freedom, and beauty, dance is sacred. It is a prayer for the future, a remembrance of the past and a joyful exclamation of thanks for the present.
– Amelia Atwater-Rhodes

CONFESSION:

I do not spend time on my knees, and I find meditation challenging since it is difficult for me to sit still and quiet my mind.

At the fundamental church I attended as a child, prayers were loud and forceful. We knelt uncomfortably on the floor, and male parishioners in good standing would pray. Once God was praised for his goodness and mercy, the begging began. They interceded to heal the sick, change the hearts of the sinners, find jobs, get someone elected to office, etc. After ten minutes or so, when the appointed one was red-faced, out of breath, and close to a heart attack, the prayer ended with "In Jesus name, Amen."

I could never understand this form of prayer. First, kneeling was like punishment or self-flagellation. Second, the same prayers were repeats. If God is all knowing and all-powerful, why is it necessary to ask for the same thing time and again? Third, I thought we were supposed to pray to the "Big Guy." Since Jesus is God's son, why did they address the second in command?

In addition, is it appropriate to intercede on someone's behalf? Unless our prayers affirm their highest good and bring about their greatest soul growth, is it ever proper to pray for a particular outcome? Do we really know what is best for others and ourselves? Could we be interfering with Divine Order when we pray for something specific? Obviously, I have many unresolved issues with prayer.

When I first started to do intuitive, energy healings, I described my process to a spiritual friend. She warned, "Don't ever do that to me unless I ask!" I thought I was doing something good, but she revealed that it was inappropriate to influence others with our intentions, even good ones, without their consent. Good lesson! Now, I focus my prayers on the person who does the asking regardless of what they ask, or for whom.

During my childhood, our family gathered in the family room for devotions every day before school or church. One of us read a passage from the Bible, and then we knelt and took turns praying aloud. Thank heavens for carpet! We mentioned friends and family members by name and asked God to protect and help them. When we had a test or musical performances, we asked for help, anything to fill a few minutes and please our parents.

One morning a cricket chirped throughout our morning prayers. It was common for critters to get into the house in the country, but this one seemed awfully close. I discovered it was in the toe of my shoe! My sisters and I started to giggle at this welcomed disruption until Dad gave us a stern look over his shoulder. But the cricket continued to mock us and with every chirp seemed to say "Blah, blah, blah."

Regular prayer time stopped when I went to college. No longer believing in a deity who bestowed favors on good little people who looked and acted the part, I left the church with its judgmental and punishing God behind. However, when crises occurred or bad things happened, I reverted to my old ways and begged for help. I felt like a hypocrite, but old habits die hard!

I remember begging for guidance when a friend struggled with emotional issues. As I speeded on the interstate to reach her as quickly as possible, I cried and pleaded for God's help, knowing my friend was in an extremely anxious state. When I arrived, I encouraged her to lie down and breathe deeply. I turned on relaxing music, sat beside her, and energetically cradled her in my arms to offer comfort. I was obviously guided to do this because within five minutes she calmed down and went to sleep. Thank you, God! Later, I ensured that she received professional help.

When I started on my spiritual journey, I took a class at the College of Metaphysics on meditation. We learned how to still our minds and sit or walk in silence. We were encouraged to say a mantra or stare at a candle, flower, or object to remain focused. These activities did little to calm my monkey mind. Instead, I felt more comfortable engaging in a contemplative form of prayer. This is how the *Blueprint* evolved. I was awakened long before dawn and lay quietly in a state of heightened awareness. Words and concepts flowed into my mind. I mentally gave thanks for these ideas, not realizing that gratitude was also a form of prayer. Through gratitude, I opened the door and connected directly with Spirit.

Years later I realized our thoughts are also prayers. The church choir sang a song before the minister prayed; "Our thoughts are prayers, and we are always praying; our thoughts are prayers, listen to what you're saying..." With every thought—both good and bad—we express our wishes. Gossip about neighbors intensifies the negativity in their lives and is like a curse. Worry about a family member only expands their pain. Complaints about poor leadership make things worse in the workplace. When we focus on the negative, we augment suffering.

OMG! When all this finally sank into my awareness, I felt a conscious shift in my thoughts from negatives to positives. Instead of worrying, I accepted what was; instead of complaining about what was wrong, I focused on the good. I put on rose-colored glasses and acted as if all was well until I genuinely believed it. And most of the time it was.

Once when a hurricane was headed in our direction, I prayed it would change course. I did not want it to damage our community and home. I received a direct order from a higher authority not to impose my will on the weather. In other words, I was told not to interfere with what was happening. This helped me learn not to waste time and energy praying for specifics. I also do not repeat prayers. I may think or say an affirming statement, then let it go because the message is out there, and I trust that all is well and in perfect Divine Order.

My intuitive healings are also a form of prayer. We begin by affirming that we are open, ready, and willing for higher guidance. During the healing process, I see the individual as pure Essence, beloved, healthy, holy, and whole. When issues, concerns, old beliefs, and blocking behaviors rise to the surface, a door opens, and a shift occurs. I know that healing is only possible when we change our perspective.

One client was stuck in a negative job and wanted to know what she should do. She appeared to be wearing cement shoes that were so heavy she could not move forward. The message was crystal clear: untie the shoes representing whatever is holding you back, and instead of searching for a new job, just show up every day "as the Presence and as Love." In other words, it does not matter where we work, what we do, or who we serve; we only need to show up as Love, Peace and Joy. This change in perception served my client very well and a new job became available within a couple of months. I find it remarkably interesting that when we stop resisting and accept what is, when we quit wanting something and keeping it at bay, the energy shifts, and blessings flow.

Unlike many religious groups, our spiritual community does not pray for world peace. Instead, we meditate on the One Presence and Power in the Universe that is known by many names. We trust God/Source/Spirit/Universe and know whatever happens is for the highest good. No begging or prayers are necessary, only gratitude. Already done!

AFFIRMATION:

In the silence and stillness, I sense the Presence of God flowing in, through, and as me. I know that all is well and in perfect Divine Order.

Day 19

From Competition to Cooperation

Moments passed while the dancers held tight to each other, as though their bodies were melting together. The expression on their features as they lifted their faces to the sky was one of unimaginable joy.
– Hannah Fielding

Confession:

I am competitive, like to win, to be first, and to do things myself because I believe I can usually do a better job than other people.

When you have four siblings, you are always competing for something because there may not be enough to go around—your parent's attention, another piece of cake, the hula hoop, window seat in the car... I cannot imagine how my mother and her ten brothers and sisters felt when they only had one chicken to share at dinnertime. They were extremely poor and endured hardships I cannot imagine.

In our culture, winning is paramount and competition is a way of life. Unless you get the highest grades, you will not be accepted into the best college and get the primo job. If girls are not pretty enough, they will not attract the strongest and most handsome husband. If their children are not smart and cute enough, they will not be admitted to the best pre-school. On and on the rivalry goes until as retirees we find ourselves hoping our golf partners will have a bad shot so we will win the match. It does not matter that money is usually not involved, only the satisfaction of succeeding.

My siblings and I spent hours playing outdoor sports. We had no TV or electronic gadgets to entertain us. We lived too far away from town to join organized teams, so the neighborhood kids gathered in the field behind our home to play soccer, hockey, baseball, basketball, and football. My father installed floodlights so his model airplane club could fly after dark. We waited until they finished flying so we could play football under the lights. It was magical.

Tackle football was our favorite. When the captains picked their teams, they encountered a dilemma—they did not know whether to pick my sisters and me first because we were so fast and agile, or whether to let the other team choose us so they could tackle us. Because church standards did not permit us to wear slacks or shorts—men's clothing and immodest attire were prohibited—we played football in dresses. I am sure the other team got quite a view. We did not care because we were determined to win!

During the winter when we were not sled riding or ice-skating, we played Ping-Pong indoors. Several older boys hung out in Dad's model airplane shop, so we had ample partners to hone our skills. The first time I played Ping-Pong with my ex, he was twenty-one and in the service. I was sixteen, and easily beat him. He never played that game with me again. Was I supposed to let him win just so he would feel good about himself?

Perhaps our competitive spirit stems from a time when we had to fight to eat and stay alive. Since they were the stronger sex, men took on the role of protectors and ensured the very survival of our species. Today these caveman tendencies continue to haunt our world. Some believe that unless the competition is squashed, they have failed. And failure means death to the ego.

Competition is not limited to the physical and social realms but also rears its ugly head in the spiritual domain. I recall participating in conversations about the level of consciousness and questionable behaviors of religious leaders. How unaware they seemed! Did I judge others to appear more enlightened?

Eventually I discovered that only the Ego evaluates and compares. Through the *Blueprint,* I learned that instead of competing, win-win-win solutions are ideal and possible. It is not good enough for both parties to compromise. Mother Earth must also triumph. Whatever we do, we must protect and sustain our fragile planet for future generations. I also believe everyone should have the opportunity to be self-sufficient and assume responsibility for his or her own well-being. No one is entitled. At the same time, we need to support those unable to care for themselves. Unless we all win, nobody does.

When I began my spiritual journey, I studied alone. I had no faith-based community and the only guidance I received was from my "inner guru." I read every spiritual book I could get my hands on but received no feedback on the *Blueprint.* I wanted and needed to know if my work was correct. It certainly seemed unique and compatible with other sacred teachings, but how was I to know for sure if I was on the right track?

Dr. David Hawkins' book, *Power vs. Force,* and his "Map of Consciousness" provided an interesting solution. I liked his premise because at that time I was still "keeping score." I asked a friend who was skilled in kinesiology to test the *Blueprint*, and sure enough, it was way up there on the scale. Nothing like a high score to make you feel gifted and blessed! Ego-Pamela was elated.

A MasterMind group provided honest, compassionate feedback. If they confirmed my ego's need to hear I was exceptional and special, they would have done a great disservice. Instead, they let me know if, and when, I was off base. This sacred circle was an amazing gift, the perfect example of how we learn and grow together. We are all equal in the eyes of God.

I designed women's groups for churches based on the ancient maternal approach of communication, cooperation, and commonality. This is the opposite of top-down hierarchies common to religions, businesses, and educational institutions. When women sit in a circle around a meaningful center or goal, all are blessed by the synergistic results. By openly sharing wisdom and working together, the entire tribe thrives. No competition or compromise is necessary.

My need to finish first finally subsided when I realized the *Blueprint* did not belong to me, but to the Universe. I was just the scribe, the vessel through which it emerged. When I sensed my oneness with others, I realized we are all in this together. If one of us evolves, we all do. As Dr. David Hawkins said, "To become more conscious is the greatest gift anyone can give to the world; moreover, in a ripple effect, the gift comes back to its source."

Fortunately, my Inner Competitor embraced this concept and stepped aside. We are all beloved children of God. Each of us has a unique purpose, special skills, and the opportunity to serve. We no longer need to do battle to survive because of our divine inheritance. There truly are enough resources in this abundant Universe for everyone. Instead of competing, we can cooperate and empower every individual to achieve his or her highest potential. In doing so, we uplift each other and all humanity.

AFFIRMATION:

I am part of the whole and live harmoniously with all Creation. I do my best in every moment to achieve my highest potential and encourage others to do the same.

DAY 20

From Resistant to Guided

To dance is to be out of yourself. Larger, more beautiful, more powerful…This is power, it is glory on earth and it is yours for the taking.
– Agnes De Mille

CONFESSION:

I usually plow ahead and do what I think needs to be done, instead of waiting to receive or follow inner guidance.

For twenty days, I have awakened an hour early to meditate and journal. Now I look forward to this morning ritual. In fact, since day three, I wake up before my alarm sounds. I cannot wait to see what emerges. I have not always been so excited about journaling. We have had an off and on relationship for many years. The first time I learned about the benefits of journaling was when I attended a creative leadership retreat. The participants were strongly encouraged to journal every day for six months. It was a chore that I dreaded and resisted. My first entries were boring descriptions of activities I had engaged in that day. On occasion, I added comments about my feelings, especially when life presented a challenge. I kept my journal in the bedside stand and wrote before going to sleep each night.

One day my stepdaughters found my journal and read what I wrote about them. I was truly angry and "blessed" them out for invading my privacy. At the same time, I was embarrassed that they discovered how I truly felt about them. I had written how one was nasty and the other needy. Prior to that pivotal moment, I had walked on eggshells. I had been overly sweet so they would accept me as part of the family.

This painful experience was a blessing in disguise. For the first time since I remarried, I no longer had to play nice, and I set some boundaries. I also made sure my writings would remain private in the future.

As I journal today, I am more open. I allow the words to flow from the depths of my being instead of from my left-brain. I do not worry what friends and family, or spiritual students will think, but am honest and transparent. This exercise is clearing my soul. I do not censor what I write and find this amazing morning ritual most helpful. I open my heart and tap into the creative flow that comes from a higher source. All I do is wait and allow Spirit to write through me. To say I have been surprised at what emerges is putting it mildly.

I have not always been open to divine guidance. Often, I was too impatient and busy to pause, ask, and listen. When I left home for college, I abandoned the ritual of daily devotions. I went through the motions as a child because I did not have a choice, but I never truly felt connected with God. Now when I pause each morning, I sense the Presence and trust its nudging's. How different my life is when I do this! I am led and supported as a higher force takes over. The words flow freely and coherently. I do not struggle and never have writer's block. Now when the Busy Worker Bee follows the guidance of the inner Queen Bee, or Essence, all is in perfect Divine Order. Everything seems easy and effortless.

For my birthday years ago, my older sister treated me to a session with an intuitive artist who saw spirit guides. She drew a medicine man with gorgeous green eyes. He had a medicine bag around his neck and later gave it to me in a vision during meditation. This extraordinary man also led me on an amazing journey 1000 years ago. After going back in time through a wormhole, I sat on the ground by a fire in the Southwest. My guide tapped me on the shoulder and motioned for me to follow him up an exceedingly high mountain. Up and up we went, pausing at intervals to rest. As we neared the top, we merged as one. Then I stepped into the Light. It was so intense, so radiant, I could not move or breathe. I was in the presence of God.

I learned something critical from this Medicine Man. Our so-called "spirit guides" are not separate beings but a part of us. They are expressions of our Higher Self, the Holy Spirit, Christ Consciousness, the Still Small Voice within, Essence, or whatever you call that sacred part of yourself. All we need to do is acknowledge its power and presence, listen, and follow its guidance. The divinity within is who and what we are. We are not physical beings with a soul, but spiritual beings expressing in the physical realm.

Years ago, I had a reading with a medium who described a past life and mentioned the kingdom of elemental beings. I had never heard of this before and when I inquired, she encouraged me to try automatic writing for the answers. She suggested I write a question, sit in silence for three minutes and write the answer that came to me.

Before trying this process, I checked online and learned nature spirits included an invisible world of tree sprites, fairies, little people, and other ethereal entities. Then I sat in the silence and asked my question. What are these beings and their significance? Did I get an earful! Here is a segment of my very first automatic writing experience:

> *Great job of personalizing Creation, the Creator, and the creative process! ...elemental beings are used by some to explain the earth's energetic essence. The so-called "little people" that are believed by some to inhabit earth and all nature are constructs of the mind. They are imaginary concepts portrayed with human features to help people understand the chaotic, evolutionary process. Fairies and devas have been devised to explain the humor and "ill-will" of creation as it continues to unfold.*

> *Once people understand that the nature of all Creation is not good or bad, not perfect or imperfect, but flowing in harmony and perfect Divine Order, then they can accept what is. No subtle forces outside of Universal Intelligence have dominion. However, it is possible through intention to make a difference. Your intentions and thoughts are the very devas and fairies that create havoc or harmony.*

WOW! As the writing continued, I learned how we project our own image onto everything. We put faces on energy that we sense around us but cannot see. Because we are human, we see angels, guides, aliens, demons, and even God with human features. These are projections. By seeing energy as separate entities, we divorce ourselves from our earthly home, from the heaven within, and from God. Only when we know oneness can we paint over the well-defined lines that define us as separate in our mistaken mental picture of reality.

Higher guidance comes from the divinity within and is always perfect. Chaos results when we are closed to this sacred council or do not follow it. When we fail to patiently wait and listen, or when we think we know better and go against the flow, we are not in harmony with the Universe. By taking the time to sit in silence and by welcoming instructions from Spirit, life is so much easier. We no longer struggle or suffer. We can choose to let go of the inner battle and embrace the truth that comes directly from the deepest, most sacred part of our being. It is always available and always correct. What a blessing!

Affirmation:

I listen to that still small voice within and follow its perfect, divine guidance.

DAY 21

From Doubt to Certainty

Life is sweet when you pay attention. When it doesn't seem sweet, put a sticker on your nose and do a funky dance.
– Whitney Scott

CONFESSION:

I have difficulty trusting others and prefer to rely only on myself to avoid disappointment.

My three sisters and I married men who were less than dependable the first time around. My ex did not support my career and, in my opinion, made many poor financial choices. During the seven years that we were destitute college students living on the GI Bill, he bought seven guns for hunting. He may have been a brilliant student and became an excellent physician, but his priorities were off. No wonder our relationship fizzled and died after a few frustrating years.

During the long ten years between marriages, I dated many tall, handsome slugs. They may have been attractive on the outside but were lacking in substance. This pattern continued until an obsessive admirer threatened my life. When I finally explored the basis for the lure of height, I discovered what I truly desired in a relationship: stability and security. Then I found the perfect partner. I am blessed to have a solid, loving relationship with an amazing, attractive man who adores me. This year we will celebrate our thirty-first anniversary and look forward to many more. My life is a testament to the fact that it is possible to let go of old habits, see more clearly, and change your life for the better!

When I met my current husband, he was so different from the typical guy I dated that I was hesitant to commit to a relationship. My older sister gave him the thumbs up, however, so I knew I had a winner. Because of my bad track record, I did not trust myself to know if he was right for me or not, but I trusted her instincts. Only then was I able to open my heart and place my faith in this wonderful man.

I learned a great deal about trust from the *Blueprint.* Trust is the basis for self-esteem and self-worth. It begins when we know we can depend on our caregivers to care for us, to be there when we need them, and protect us from harm. Despite their shortcomings and rigid religious beliefs, I am fortunate to have had responsible, reliable parents.

When I was seven, I stepped on a wasp. Immediately, I swelled up like a balloon. My eyes swelled shut and my foot was the size of a softball. I was hysterical and had difficulty breathing. Fortunately, my grandmother was home and drove my mother and me to the Emergency Room. At that time, Mother did not have a driver's license. Her family was extremely poor and had no car, so she had not yet learned how to drive. When I almost died from anaphylactic shock, she decided it was time. She let go of her fears and took to the wheel. She did everything possible to be trustworthy and to keep us safe.

Once we learn that we can trust others, we can internalize this ability and transform it into self-trust and self-reliance. By making choices that are in our highest good, we create desired results and learn to trust ourselves. We become trustworthy as others discover they can also trust us.

I became an instant mother when I married thirty years ago. Although my stepdaughters were teenagers, I still felt a sense of responsibility and wanted to be there for them. Their mother had died almost three years before their father married me and the trauma still haunted them. The youngest feared that, I too, would leave them and they would face another painful loss. It took a long time, but our girls learned I was trustworthy and that they could confide in me. I am still here for them and have remained a stable force for many years.

Although I had no experience as a parent, I have done my best to support and encourage our girls. When the youngest graduated from college with a degree in psychology and could not find work in her field, she was at a loss. She did not know what to do and feared her father would be disappointed if she did not use her education. I reminded her that all we wanted was for her to be happy and gainfully employed. Then I asked what she liked to do. She enjoyed working out with a personal trainer, so I suggested she find out how he became certified. Within two months, she and I were on a plane to Atlanta so she could attend her first workshop. Today she has a beautiful studio and a thriving Pilates and personal training business.

I have a friend who does not trust herself to make decisions. She blames her lack of ability on older sisters who made all the decisions when they were growing up. She usually waits or vacillates until someone else makes a move and she has no choice but to react. Instead of being confident and proactive, her options become limited. Fear and distrust prevent her from taking risks and embracing opportunities that arise.

Perhaps instead of trusting ourselves, we should rely on a higher power. When we trust God and the Universe to guide and provide, we need not worry. With trust, we do not focus on what is missing but embrace what is and see all as good. Then, our cup overflows with abundance and we have nothing to fear. We are certain. We know in our bones what is true and what is a construct of the mind.

All we need to succeed is a little encouragement and belief in ourselves. By first trusting in our parents, we learn to trust ourselves and make decisions in our best interest. Then we become trustworthy in fulfilling our social and professional responsibilities. With confidence and faith, we are no longer subject to the criticisms and whims of others. We stand up for ourselves and do our best.

When we trust ourselves, others, and God, we gratefully and graciously accept our abundant divine inheritance. We operate from a positive stance on the assumption that all is well. We let go of past disappointments and unfulfilled expectations so we can enjoy every moment of every day. We will never forget pain from the past, but with forgiveness, our wounds will heal. They will no longer limit us or keep us from expressing the truth of our being. With trust, we can let go of victimhood and realize our highest potential as beloved expressions of God.

Affirmation:

I trust myself and I trust God, and know the Universe provides all that I need to thrive and live a meaningful, productive life.

DAY 22

From Rigid to Flexible

The only way to make sense out of change is to plunge into it, move with it, and join the dance.
– Alan W. Watts

CONFESSION:

I resist changing my routine but am impatient with others who seem inflexible.

I have a comfortable routine. I rise early to meditate and journal, then walk, exercise, have breakfast, edit my writings, eat lunch, swim, shower, run errands, fix dinner, relax, watch TV, read, then sleep. This may sound boring, but a schedule helps me to remain focused on priorities. When necessary, I alter the sequence to accommodate appointments, visits with family and friends, social and spiritual gatherings, leisure pursuits, etc. If changes are required, I prefer advanced notice. I also schedule important appointments before mid-afternoon since I am a morning person and run out of steam by dinnertime.

Regardless of schedules, when a crisis occurs, we rise to the occasion and do what needs to be done. Years ago, my husband was recognized for his quick response while attending a business expo to promote his new car wash. He noticed smoke rising from the vent of a Port-a-Potty, grabbed a bucket of water and put out the fire. For his efforts, he received the "Johnny on the Spot" award.

Changes are not always short-term or amusing. When my father had a stroke at fifty-eight and was paralyzed on the left side, he could no longer fly model airplanes, one of his greatest joys. He also needed a great deal of help with activities of daily living. Mother became his primary caregiver and adjusted her entire life to accommodate his disability. She took care of him for over twenty-one years before he died. I have no idea how she found the strength and endurance.

I learned a valuable lesson about change at the Center for Creative Leadership. When a situation requires action, we have four options. Some are more effective than others are. The chart below shows these choices with their productivity and stress levels.

WHINE Low Productivity High Stress	**CONFRONT** High Productivity High Stress
DO NOTHING Low Productivity Low Stress	**ADAPT** High Productivity Low Stress

As the play on words suggests, "shift happens." Good and bad things occur regardless of our efforts to control them, and our only option is to choose how we respond. Ideally, we adapt and change in harmony with what is. When we accept the inevitable and quit swimming against the current, we experience less stress. The outcome is also more effective.

However, going with the flow is easier said than done. Our brains have neural pathways that make us automatically repeat patterns. It takes at least twenty-one repetitions to create a new "groove" in our brain and adopt a new habit. No wonder change is so difficult! We must consistently go against the grain to change our ways.

We have all heard that change is good. Perhaps it keeps us on our toes and keeps our minds sharp and malleable. Without altering our choices, we would rot in a rut and fail to experience life in its fullness. If we do not embrace opportunities that arise, we can miss moments of happiness and meaningful experiences. If we repeat the same things, we will never evolve. We will continue behaviors that cause stress, discomfort, and pain. According to Albert Einstein, "doing the same thing over and over again and expecting different results" is the very definition of insanity.

To experience positive change, we need a well-defined goal and plan of action fueled by motivation and perseverance. Without courage and determination, we will not successfully alter our ways. Since this is day twenty-two of my journaling exercise, I trust this transformative practice has become a new habit and I will stick with it to fulfill my higher purpose more effectively and efficiently.

I heard a story about a woman who had great difficulty making changes despite the consequences. She walked down a road and fell in a hole. She climbed out and the next day did the same thing. She saw the hole on her third trip but fell in anyway. On the fourth day, she paused at the edge, but was unable to stop herself. The fifth day she walked around the hole to avoid falling in, but on the last day finally took another street—new path, no pitfalls!

This perfectly illustrates how difficult it is to alter our routine. We continue the same custom even though roadblocks interfere with our intentions. Ideally, we will get the message and take a new path before repeating painful mistakes and enduring unnecessary hardships. Those who repeat old patterns are either unable or unwilling to consider their options. With their head in the sand, they fail to realize that change is inevitable, and it is usually good.

I recently watched a documentary about Peace Pilgrim. What a dynamic person! She gave up everything, including her identity, to walk around the country for twenty-eight years and spread the word about peace. She did not stop walking until she died suddenly in a car accident just before her seventy-third birthday. She made over twenty trips across the country and kept track of how far she walked until she reached 25,000 miles. She never accepted or carried any money, slept only when offered a bed, and ate only when food was provided. This amazing woman changed her life and became a perfect expression of inner peace. No doubt, she also had a great impact on countless others and will continue to do so through her writings and example.

The Lord's Prayer includes the phrase, "on earth, as it is in heaven." This means that change first occurs inside of us and illustrates the Law of Mind Action: "As within, so without." In other words, if we want to make a difference in the world, if we want world peace, we must first change our perspectives, our behaviors, and ourselves. Although we can only change ourselves, positive shifts in our consciousness can uplift all humanity through our energetic connection. What a blessing to know we do not have to fix others or solve the problems of the world. All we must do is change ourselves!

Affirmation:

I make positive changes in my perceptions and my behaviors, knowing that as I adapt, I uplift humanity and change the world from within.

DAY 23

From Over-Extended to Rested

Dancing is surely the most basic and relevant of all forms of expression. Nothing else can so effectively give outward form to an inner experience.
– Lyall Watson

CONFESSION:

I did not want to get up this morning. Although I am committed to this process, I need to recharge my inner batteries.

This is the first time I slept until my alarm clock rang since day three of this forty-day process. To make matters worse, I awakened in the middle of a weird dream and felt out of sorts. I should not be tired because I went to bed early and enjoyed a relaxing massage yesterday. The therapist worked on some knots in my shoulders and upper back caused from all the writing and computer work.

I am not surprised that I need a break since I have been on an energy-high for the past few months. Like everyone, I need some downtime. Even God took a day of rest on the seventh day in the creation story.

I remember Sundays when I was growing up. We took the fourth Commandment—Remember the Sabbath day to keep it holy—very seriously. For some reason, it was interpreted by our religious leaders as "Thou shalt not do anything fun on Sundays." We were not permitted to buy anything, work, eat out, ride bikes, play sports, or do anything active. We had to be quiet because our folks always took an "afternoon nap."

I could never understand all the Sunday rules. Isn't doing the dishes work? Isn't the minister working when he preaches? Is enjoying life irreverent? And when is the actual Sabbath? We worship on Sunday. Other religions believe Sabbath is on Saturday to be consistent with the seventh day of creation. Still others observe Sabbath on Friday evenings. Does it really matter when the Sabbath is? Surely, our religious leaders do not believe that our calendar coincides with the actual "days" of Creation.

Despite all the no-no's, our Sundays were quite busy. We went to Sunday school in the morning and stayed for a lengthy sermon, then went back to church in the evening for a youth program and another service where the minister spoke a second time. This meant we sat on hard, uncomfortable pews and listened to preachers and teachers for over four hours every Sunday. To say it was exhausting is putting it mildly.

My perspective on Sabbath is far different today. It is far more than a day of rest and worship. Every moment becomes sacred. We are spiritual beings enjoying a physical experience. Within us is a spark of the Divine that perpetually permeates all Creation. When we recognize and embrace our divinity and know our Oneness with All That Is, we are more aware. Instead of dedicating one day to spiritual studies, Sabbath becomes far more than a day or weekly ritual. It is a continuous state of mind that reflects the Essence of our being.

When we are aware of the constant loving presence of God, we enjoy higher consciousness and a reverence for life as it unfolds. We honor every person that crosses our path and recognize that each encounter is holy. We do not need a special day of the week to pause and remember this. Sabbath is observed every time we pause in the silence and go within. In this sacred space, we bring our thoughts, feelings, and actions into alignment with the truth of our being. When we integrate teachings and allow them to become who we are, we realize our potential as an expression of God. Sabbath makes this possible.

Day 23

Perhaps this is what my extended "rest" was all about last winter and spring. While I was recovering from several health issues, all I could do was rest. I had no energy and was unable to fulfill my many roles and responsibilities. This downtime was an unexpected blessing. I shifted out of a "doing" mode into a "being" mode. I resigned from all my projects and commitments and was free to refocus on my own work. Since then, I have been on a high. An abundance of divine energy flows around and through me. Although I am compelled to continue this ambitious writing exercise, I know I receive as much rest as I need. A force far greater than my own physical strength sustains me. I have also found a balance between active times and restful periods.

I usually awaken early full of energy and begin my morning ritual. I light a candle and pause to center myself in the silence. When guidance comes, I pick up my pen and journal. This is how I observe Sabbath each day. As I refocus on my connection with Spirit, I experience a sacred moment. In the Presence, I recommit to living in harmony with the truth of my being. Another benefit from this morning ritual is that my day goes more smoothly, and my work flows effortlessly and easily.

Rest, also a form of Sabbath, is important for a balanced life. We need sleep to restore the proteins in our brains. This is critical for our survival and for us to function optimally. I am thrilled to be sleeping well these days because I struggled with insomnia while going through menopause. Not everyone is as lucky in the sleep department and are dependent on sleep aids. Some have sleep apnea and need to wear uncomfortable devices to bed. Others may sleep well but keep everyone else awake "sawing logs." Regardless, we all will sleep better if we heal relationships and turn stressors and worries over to God before we close our eyes.

With adequate rest, we should have enough energy to last the entire day. However, as we get older our activity level and sleep requirements change. If we can no longer sustain a high level of activity, we may need to take refreshing naps. The key is to listen to the body, become aware of what it is telling us, and rest when needed.

Sabbath also represents the final stage of life. As youth and young adults, we were busy working and raising a family. But as seniors, we slow down and enjoy the fruits of our labors. We take time to ponder our past and review the impact of our efforts. As we get ready for bed each evening, we can thoughtfully examine our activities of the day and determine if we have been purposeful and productive. Are we leaving a legacy of love for our children and grandchildren?

Sabbath is not just about going to church. It can be observed as a day of the week, a ritual, a period of rest, a way of being, or a stage of life. We only need to realize that every minute, every person, every encounter, and everything in our lives is sacred. With greater awareness we also realize that the most holy times are quiet, solitary times with Spirit. Instead of feeling lonely, we find comfort in Oneness and know that no matter what is going on in the world around us, all is well.

AFFIRMATION:

I rest in the Presence and know that every person, experience, and moment in my life is sacred.

Day 24

From Tedious Work to Joyful Expression

You dance love, and you dance joy, and you dance dreams.
– Gene Kelly

Confession:

I always find the easiest and quickest way to complete my work; in fact, I would rather focus on what gives me joy instead of work.

I would rather not work if I do not have to. As teenagers, my sisters and I felt like slaves. We worked nonstop and did most of the cleaning, cooking, laundry, yard work, and gardening. Before we could play with our friends, we had to dig a bucket of Dandelions from the yard. Before we could have a picnic and lay out in the sun, we had to pick a basket of berries. We picked, washed, chopped, and froze vegetables and fruit before we could swim in the creek.

From our perspective, our younger brother did not do his fair share. My sisters and I made his bed, picked up his toys, and did his laundry while he played with airplanes or earned an hourly wage working for Dad's construction business. From this, we learned that women are servants and men have all the fun.

Since work always came first, Miss Efficiency emerged and figured out ways to lighten the load. When possible, I invited a cousin or neighbor for a visit.

They arrived just in time to help with chores before playtime. I also learned that if I hung my dad's work clothes as soon as the dryer stopped, I did not have to iron them.

While married to my first husband, I did all the cleaning, laundry, and cooking like the good little wife I was trained to be. On Saturday mornings, I sent him packing while I worked my buns off. When he returned four hours later, our apartment was spick and span. After we were divorced, I discovered I only had to clean once a month because my apartment stayed nice and clean. Obviously, my ex was not only the primary source of unpleasantness in my life, but also created most of the dirt.

When my second husband proposed, I hesitated. We had avoided discussing the "M" word. I assumed that when the time came, I would move into his home. I was working full-time and wanted to make sure my workload did not increase. Before I responded to his proposal I asked, "What do you expect from a wife?" He was taken aback, but indicated he expected me to be faithful and to love him. I smiled and said I only wanted to make sure he was not going to discontinue his cleaning service. With his promise to keep them on board, I eagerly said, "Yes." Our agreement stands to this day. Other than mopping the kitchen floor once in a long while, I do not clean.

When I retired from my last fulltime professional position, my husband was creating a new business. I had extra time on my hands, so I helped more with grocery shopping, cooking, and laundry. To protect his clothing from wear and tear, my husband always hung his T-shirts and polo shirts in the basement to dry, then ironed them. When I took over this task, I discovered an easier way to get the wrinkles out. I fluffed them in the dryer and folded them when he was not around.

Months later my husband caught me as I smoothed, folded, and stacked a pile of shirts. When he asked what I was doing, I replied, "Ironing." Then I confessed that I had been doing this for quite a while. He was amused and even bought a steamer. Then I never had to get the iron or ironing board out of the closet again. He had no choice but to adapt to my work methods unless he wanted to pay for ironing services.

Cleaning seemed like a waste of time and energy to me, but two of my sisters enjoy cleaning and even find it therapeutic. Perhaps it is a form of meditation—a way to be in the moment. Scrub floors, wash windows—no thought. I much prefer activities that stimulate the brain and allow creativity to flow. Most of my professional positions have been inspiring and in perfect harmony with my talents because I designed them. I enjoyed working because it was meaningful, and I was able to help others. With timelines to keep me on schedule, coworkers to lend their expertise, and staff to assist, we accomplished a great deal.

When I retired early, I was on my own and not prepared for the challenges of solo work. I did not have access to feedback, marketing support, or distribution systems. I was accountable to only myself. Since deadlines were arbitrary, I procrastinated. Instead of focusing on my own work, I became a professional volunteer, implementing projects for many organizations. Although I received a lot of satisfaction, experience, and gratitude for my efforts, it never felt fulfilling. Unless I am writing, doing healings, facilitating a workshop, or giving a presentation about the *Blueprint,* I feel I am not living purposefully. The *Blueprint* is my life work, my priority, my reason for being. It guided my evolution, and I am committed to sharing it with others.

I faced another challenge that interfered with my productivity—extreme energy swings. I was not able to maintain a steady work pace; I either worked like a maniac night and day or lay in bed like a blob. I rode the pendulum from one extreme to the other and never knew when my energy would shift. While I was down, I felt guilty for being lazy. I learned as a child to believe that a strong work ethic was synonymous with goodness and a requirement for entry into the pearly gates.

I finally found balance once I realized my energy swings were related to diet, allergies, thyroid, and blood pressure. I have also discovered a better way to work. Instead of having an all-or-none approach, I enjoy a steady, slower pace. I work three to four hours a day and reserve energy for playtime with family and friends. I put myself first. I eat right, exercise every day, and meditate each morning before work. Through meditation, I tap into the infinite source of energy and no longer need to rely totally on myself to make things happen. I show up and allow Spirit to work through, and as, me.

To be honest, my work feels more like play because I am so passionate about it. I have found what I love and come alive when I can share the *Blueprint*. Friends say I literally glow, and my eyes sparkle when I talk about it. For this amazing gift, I am most grateful. For the opportunity to pay it forward, I am ecstatic.

When I share the *Blueprint* and healing energy, I am productive, purposeful, and make a positive difference. The fact that I have generated little income to date does not matter. I abundantly receive so many other things for my efforts. Sharing spiritual wisdom and practical guidance from the *Blueprint* is not work. It is not my job, but my joy.

Affirmation:

I embrace every opportunity to share my time, talents, and treasures in a meaningful way to uplift humanity.

Day 25

From Outward Appearance to Inner Being

When you dance, you can enjoy the luxury of being you.
–Paulo Coelho

Confession:

I have always been more concerned about how I look than who I am.

When I was a young girl, Mother made new dresses for every occasion. She may have dressed my sisters and me alike, but we had a new outfit for the first day of school, Thanksgiving, Christmas, Valentine's Day, Easter, etc. Every time we sang in a concert, we sported a new dress. I am still tempted to buy an outfit for every event, complete with matching shoes, jewelry, and a hat.

I recently spoke with a dear friend who at eighty-five is tired of dressing up for everyone. She is weary after performing the part of dutiful wife and mother for many years. Her husband recently passed and now she is trying to discover who she really is. She feels that she played roles so long she has no idea what is important to her. Until now, she never came first and always felt she needed to impress others with her appearance.

Through the *Blueprint* I have learned a great deal about who I am, but I still jump through hoops to look the part and play the many roles in my life—wife, daughter, stepmother, program planner, neighbor, friend, speaker, author, and teacher. I know that I am a spiritual being but am still concerned about how I appear. I am proud to be back in shape, but do not like the wrinkles that are becoming more prominent on my face. Despite the inevitable changes, I am determined to age gracefully. I have resisted the urge to dye my hair but wonder how I will feel as the aging process accelerates, and the additional years leave their marks on my body.

When my husband and I first moved to Southwest Florida, we attended a community gathering to meet new neighbors. My husband went for refreshments, met an interesting couple, and brought them to me for introductions. We instantly connected, so we invited them back to our home to continue our discussion. I learned the gentleman and I shared similar experiences growing up in strict religious environments. I told them about my spiritual path, my doctorate in holistic health sciences, and the *Blueprint*. Our new friend shook her head in disbelief. She assumed when she met me that I was arm candy—that because I was younger and wore a cute cocktail dress, my husband chose an airhead trophy wife the second time he married. She vowed never to judge someone by his or her looks again because she had been so wrong about me.

Yesterday a friend shared an email that is a classic example of why we should not judge a book by its cover. A new minister of a 10,000+-member church dressed like a homeless man to see what the reaction would be from his new congregation. He was ignored and avoided. No one gave him any money when he said he was hungry and asked for a quarter to buy food. He tried to sit in the front of the church and the ushers made him move to the back. Later, when he was introduced, this insightful minister walked to the front of the church and quoted Matthew 25:35-40.

> *For I was hungry and you gave me something to eat, I was thirsty and you gave me something to drink, I was a stranger and you invited me in, I needed clothes and you clothed me, I was sick and you looked after me, I was in prison and you came to visit me.' Then the righteous will*

> *answer him, 'Lord, when did we see you hungry and feed you, or thirsty and give you something to drink? When did we see you a stranger and invite you in, or needing clothes and clothe you? When did we see you sick or in prison and go to visit you?' The King will reply, 'Truly I tell you, whatever you did for one of the least of these brothers and sisters of mine, you did for me.*

The congregation was in tears. What a tough lesson! We all have a great deal to learn to correct our tendency to judge by appearances.

Several years ago, we heard Neil Donald Walsh speak about his life before he became a popular spiritual author. He lost his family, job, and home and was on the street. He described how impossible it is for the homeless to find employment with their challenging circumstances. They have difficulty getting a bath, clean clothing, phone calls and mail to confirm appointments, transportation to and from interview sites, etc. His entire homeless community came to his aid so he could get a job and he never forgot it.

From that moment on, I stopped judging, and now I feel deep compassion for those who stand along the street with a sign asking for help. I no longer assume that if they really wanted to work and put forth a little more effort, a job would be available. I now give them a donation and a blessing. I also say a prayer of gratitude because I realize that if circumstances had been different, that could be me in their dirty clothes and worn-out shoes. In fact, since we are one, that homeless person is you and me.

What we wear reflects how we feel about ourselves. Some wear only name brands and the latest fashions. Others are comfortable with classic lines and timeless styles. Those who are self-conscious may wear subdued colors, while flamboyant types, like me, prefer bright colors and flashy accessories. I usually augment my outfits with one of my 200+ hats. I once read an article that claimed wearing a hat is the height of exhibitionism. I love hats, feel comfortable in them, and wear them so often that people do not recognize me without one. Maybe they are my disguise and I feel conspicuous bare headed.

Regardless of our style or preferences, clothing reflects our self-worth and self-esteem. As a child, I did not have a choice since my sisters and I wore identical hand-made outfits and looked nothing like other kids our age. We were embarrassed and wanted to fit in with our peers.

When I was a freshman in college, I wrote an English composition on "Doing Your Own Thing." I expressed my opinion that since most college students dressed like hippies, "their thing" seemed to be just like everyone else's and was not unique. During the critique, a fellow student slammed my composition, not for the writing style, creativity, or structure, but for the content. He vehemently disagreed with my position and even criticized what I wore. He attacked me for looking different and for siding with the establishment. Although I wrote this piece in jest, after looking like my sisters for years, the last thing I wanted to do was to look like everyone else.

Being in vogue is irrelevant. What we wear or how we appear to others does not matter. Only what is on the inside counts. We are all beloved children of God, all beautiful and perfect expressions of the Divine. When we can see beyond the reflection in the mirror, we know the truth of our being. When we look deep into the eyes of those we meet and see their inner spirit, we no longer feel separate. Let us gaze at each other with eyes of love, looking beyond appearances, to know only Essence and Oneness.

Affirmation:

I see beyond outward appearances and know the truth of my being.

Day 26

From Limitations to Highest Potential

I do not try to dance better than anyone else. I only try to dance better than myself.
– Mikhail Baryshnikov

Confession:

I either doubt myself and my capacity to live up to my potential or set myself up to fail with unrealistic expectations.

To say I lived a sheltered life in my younger years is putting it mildly. I was the picture of innocence and naïveté. I was raised in a small-town in the foothills of Pennsylvania. How small was it? We had no traffic lights, no industry, and no entertainment—unless you call going to one of the five churches exciting. Our town's only services included a volunteer fire company, library, and a mom-and-pop grocery. Many of the 500 residents in this village and surrounding farms were related. Since we had no TV in our home, we were isolated and had no idea of what was going on beyond the ten-to-fifteen-mile radius around us. In other words, the world of my youth was the size of a pea.

While a high school student, I was unaware of the race riots, and I never met an African American or Hispanic person until I went to college. Although I was a pen pal to a Vietnam Veteran while he was in the service, and later married him, I was unaware of what occurred on foreign soil and with the protests at home. I did not see footage of the conflicts and was ignorant of the impact it had on our returning soldiers. I lived in a fantasy world, a strict religious la-la land.

My only role models were homemakers, secretaries, missionaries, teachers, and nurses. Although our father had a thriving construction business, my sisters and I were overlooked when he decided to step back and let younger men take the reins. This was also the pattern in our church. Religious doctrine limited women to performing religious music, teaching Sunday school, or being the wife of a missionary or minister. We could never preach or be ordained.

Since I had no idea what the possibilities were, my perspective and vision for the future were as narrow as my background. I was expected to marry and have children. After all, God-fearing women were supposed to be fruitful and multiply. However, Mother was brilliant when she encouraged us to get an education—just in case a tragedy occurred, and we needed to support ourselves. The desire for a rewarding career was not a consideration.

I do not remember being praised for accomplishments or encouraged to achieve. Completing chores and being a good little girl were more important. Today, kids receive rewards just for showing up. Whether they excel or not seems irrelevant. Their parents and teachers are far more concerned with self-esteem than skill development. No one told us we were loved, special, and important. Instead, we felt like indentured servants and did what we were told. Add religious beliefs about unworthiness and you get a shy, inhibited, and insecure high school graduate with a limited view of the future.

When I finally went to college, I discovered the possibilities were endless. For the first time I was exposed to other cultures and beliefs systems. I met women in positions of power and with exciting careers. My eyes were opened to the opportunities, and I pursued a new path, one that was not limited to an unsupportive husband, housework, and babies.

While in nursing school, I also discovered I had potential. One professor gave me a "B" for a ten-credit clinical course. I thought I was doing well, but received no feedback throughout the semester, so I was unaware of her perceptions or expectations. When I asked why I received a B, she told me I was an excellent caregiver, and she would choose me as her nurse if the need ever arose. However, she believed I had far more potential. She expected more of me than the average student. She told me I was smart enough to excel and should work harder.

From that moment on, I became an over-achiever and did far more than other students. My grades went from above average to excellent and I aced my nursing boards. After graduation, one opportunity led to another, and my career blossomed—until I collapsed from exhaustion and illness.

While employed by the American Cancer Society I worked day and night, but never seemed able to complete my projects. I traveled non-stop assisting staff and volunteers with programs, often on my own time since there were not enough hours in the day. After a forced respite due to a severe upper respiratory infection, I spoke with my supervisor about my dilemma. He did not say a word, but shared an article entitled, "Where Does Your Work Come From?" What a revelation to discover my work came from me!

In that "ah-ha" moment, I realized I had transformed from a clueless country bumpkin into a workaholic with unrealistic expectations. To make matters worse, my idealistic goals were self-imposed. I set myself up to fail! After a sheltered childhood filled with fear, I chased every opportunity that came my way until I ran myself into the ground. I desperately needed balance.

Since awareness is the first step to achieving equilibrium, I became more conscious of my goals and workload. I divided "TO DO" lists into "NEED TO DOs" and "NICE TO DOs." With a little guidance from Eckhart Tolle's book, *The Power of Now*, I also learned to live in the present. Instead of focusing on the future or dwelling on past mistakes, I began to enjoy the process. Getting a job done as fast and efficiently as possible was no longer my primary objective. I also changed my perspective on my life and my work.

I maximized strengths, minimized weaknesses, and became more judicious about how I spent my time, talents, and energy. Instead of striving for lofty ideals, I learned to do my best and was happy with the results.

The challenges I face today are different. I walk between the worlds, balancing earthly commitments and roles with the spiritual aspect of life. I am learning how to be in this world, but not of it. Instead of striving to "get there" and succeed, I recognize my Divinity and express it every moment of every day. I live without limitations because the Universe provides. I have everything I need to realize my highest potential. I embrace all that I am. I have no doubts or fears as I joyfully and confidently do my best.

Affirmation:

I transform limitations and challenges into opportunities and use each one to realize my highest potential as an expression of the Divine.

DAY 27

From Failures to Opportunities

We think to dance, and dance in thought. But to hibernate in the mind, is to bring upon us an apocalypse of the Soul.
– Ilyas Kassam

CONFESSION:

I am still haunted by the times I failed or was less than effective in my efforts.

Ego-Pamela does not like to fail. She tries ridiculously hard to create ideal programs and give excellent presentations. According to the Enneagram system of self-discovery, she is a Three, a "succeeder." If anyone criticizes or complains, she is crushed. Of course, we cannot help if we fail on occasion. In fact, if we do not, it means we did not set our standards high enough or challenge ourselves. Failure is an important part of the learning curve.

I remember times when I was less than effective in my professional career. Once I was asked to speak on a topic that was outside my area of expertise. I did the research and wrote a presentation, but my delivery was not dynamic. I had to follow my notes too closely and I was low on energy. I had made a detour to have dinner with a handsome friend on the way and arrived late the night before the conference. The next morning, I did not wake up early enough to rehearse and I was not well rested. I was not asked to speak again for a while, but when I was, I made sure that I was prepared and that my priorities were straight.

Another poor performance was at a workshop for staff. The executive insisted I focus on community needs analysis and the program planning process, so I prepared a 4-hour session with exercises on these topics. When I met with his staff, they expressed different needs. Instead of changing gears, I continued in accordance with the executive's instructions. I should have followed my own guidance and completed my own needs analysis with the staff in the first place. I never made that mistake again either!

Ten years ago, I was asked to fill in for a luncheon speaker for a community women's organization. Since my talks are usually spiritual in nature, I toned it down so I would not offend anyone. My presentation was a dud. I could tell I was not inspired or inspiring when a woman at the table in front of me started to snore. Typically, my audiences are engaged and entertained. Looking back, I am not surprised at the outcome or reaction. Since we had company, I skipped my meditation that morning. Instead of allowing Spirit to guide my talk, fear forced me to whitewash my content. Now I always make sure I am mentally prepared and in the right spiritual state before I speak or conduct a workshop.

Each of these experiences taught me something valuable and I never made the same mistake twice. When we learn our lessons, failure becomes a positive experience. It took Thomas Edison many times to create the light bulb, but instead of getting discouraged, he never gave up. He said, "I have not failed; I have just learned 10,000 ways that won't work." Unless we try, fail, and try again, we will not succeed.

Failure hurts. Ego takes a beating, and we lose "face." Our very soul feels diminished. Ego may have been crushed, but failure serves another valuable purpose. It keeps us humble and reminds us that we are human. From these embarrassing experiences, we discover the importance of trying harder. We are compelled to explore different approaches and augment our repertoire. In the process, we also expand our minds and develop new skills. Not only do we grow, but we also develop compassion for others who may be less than effective.

A young friend is in the Army Reserves and recently returned from summer camp with a couple of medals. While there, she did so well she was quickly promoted to platoon leader and then company leader. For her excellent efforts and hard work, she received a four-day pass. Then she lost her key card. The sergeant almost revoked her benefits and demoted her, but a commander reminded him of all her accomplishments and his own shortcomings in the past. Fortunately, the sergeant reconsidered, and this young woman was not penalized for a breach of conduct. One slipup like this could compromise a career and the lives of fellow soldiers. No doubt, she will be more conscientious about keeping track of valuables in the future.

As we mature, we usually loosen up and become easier on others and ourselves. With a few *faux pas* under our belts, we learn to take things in stride. We realize that we do not need to beat up on ourselves for days on end for minor infractions. When we let ourselves off the hook, we can extend the same consideration to others. Instead of expecting and demanding perfection, we go with the flow. We need not prove anything to anyone or lose our self-respect. Since most of our errors are not life threatening, a mistake will not launch World War III.

One of my common blunders is the lack of follow-through. I try to do what I promise, but may run out of time, steam, or focus. My *Create CommuniTea*™ project is a classic example. I helped launch a women's higher tea circle in one church and facilitated it for six years. While working with a second church, I packaged the materials and offered them to other organizations for a reasonable fee. I promoted this program at a couple church conferences and sold six additional packages.

Unfortunately, I have not sustained my marketing and follow-up efforts. At this point, I am not even sure if the churches that purchased my program have successfully implemented and sustained them. I dropped the ball to pursue a new endeavor. It has been so long since I have been in touch that I am too embarrassed to contact the churches. Maybe this confession will renew my resolve to give this project the attention it deserves and keep the initiative going.

Why are we so affected by failure? Ego measures its worth by our successes and the kudos we receive for them. It is dependent on positive outcomes and believes it deserves the self-flagellation we bestow on ourselves for blunders. If we are rejected for being ineffective, the fragile Ego receives a mortal blow. It takes a hit every time we make an error and especially if the word gets out. Now I know these hard knocks may be for the best.

I used to rely excessively and exclusively on Ego and my own steam to accomplish earthly goals. From the *Blueprint,* I learned how to work with divine support. Instead of relying totally on Pamela to get the job done and do it right the first time, I trust higher guidance. I set my mind on the right frequency and tune in to the all-knowing, all-powerful Source and infinite supply. I listen when it prods me to notice something or try a new approach.

From this place of openness and awareness, Ego recedes, and Essence takes over. I relax and allow creative ideas to emerge easily and effectively. I do not struggle or strain. Everything flows beautifully and harmoniously. This is happening right now as I continue my forty-days of confessions. I step aside and let Spirit do its perfect work through me. I am the vessel through which God expresses.

I am so grateful for the lessons I have learned from my failures and for the grace to pick myself up and keep moving forward. It is all good and I am a better person for going through these transforming experiences.

Affirmation:

I embrace my mistakes and see my failures as opportunities to learn and evolve, knowing they are critical for my soul growth.

Day 28

From Addiction to Freedom

Caution not spirit, let it roam wild; for in that natural state dance embraces divine frequency.
– Shah Asas Rizvi

Confession:

I am addicted to sweets, praise, acceptance, and becoming enlightened.

Isn't it interesting that we often crave things that are not good for us? Take food for example. I love sweets, especially chocolate, and the richer and gooier the better! At the same time, I am allergic to corn and wheat, which is an ingredient in nearly every dessert and candy. For some bizarre reason, the body craves that which it cannot tolerate. A demented entity seems to reside within, growling loudly and incessantly, "FEED ME!" like the flesh-eating plant from the play "Little Shop of Horrors."

Fortunately, I have learned to live without processed sugar and my body seems satisfied with natural and healthy treats of fruits and nuts. I still have a sweet tooth and if tempted, I could easily dive headfirst into a vat of velvety smooth chocolate, so I need to be vigilant to maintain a healthy lifestyle. My sweet addiction could easily have created a major health issue had I not changed my ways and gotten back in shape. My blood sugar was creeping up, and with a diagnosis of hypoglycemia and a family history of diabetes, no doubt I would have been diabetic very soon. Now my blood levels are well within normal limits.

I have never been addicted to cigarettes, alcohol, drugs, or sex, but know others who have struggled to give up highly addictive habits. A friend's husband tried unsuccessfully for years to live without drugs. He made promise after promise to change his ways and broke his word every time. When their children were young and he was responsible on occasion for their care, he would disappear. Days later, he would make a desperate call from jail or a crack house, begging to come home, pleading for forgiveness. It took weeks for him to recuperate after a binge. A few months later, the destructive pattern was repeated.

Because my friend was as addicted to him as he was to drugs, she always welcomed her husband back. She prayed and trusted God would heal him of his disease. She believed her husband's false promises and good intentions. After twenty years, she finally divorced him and now enjoys a far more peaceful, happy life. She was also surprised to discover that when she stopped enabling him, he was able to heal from his addiction.

Physical addictions are just one temptation we face. The ego also craves fewer tangible treats that give us an emotional and mental high. Ego-Pamela is addicted to praise because it makes her feel special, important, and loved. She wants and needs to know that others see what a great job she has done and that she is gifted and effective. There is nothing wrong with developing and using our talents, but Ego insists that others know about every one of them. The more others become aware of our skills and successes, the more bloated the ego becomes and the more we do to generate these "well-deserved" accolades.

Ego-Pamela also needs to be right. I remember the first day I attended a psychology class during my last year of nursing school. I had transferred from the University of Pittsburgh to Widener University to be close to where my ex was attending medical school. As a newbie, I knew no one. The other students had been together for three years and had developed close friendships. When the professor asked a question, I responded with an incorrect answer. I was so embarrassed I know my face was fifty shades of red. After class, one student came over to welcome me and I blew him off. We later became good friends, but because I felt so diminished by one silly error, I was not open to his expression of kindness on that very first day.

When we are incorrect and others know about it, Ego feels shame. It is so attached to the need to be right that we feel less than adequate. We believe we are less than whole if we fall short of our unrealistic expectations. How sad!

Ego-Pamela has another addiction—she wants to be first. She needs to be first at the start and first to cross the finish line. Once, in a dream, I lined up for a race. I snuck around the side and jumped ahead to get an early start. When the coach spotted me, I had to go to the back of the group and start over. I got the message, but my tendency to start first is well ingrained. I am Miss Efficiency and am compelled to figure out how to get the job done in the shortest time using the least amount of energy. If I am loading the dishwasher, I must do it more efficiently than anyone else. If I am folding laundry, baking cookies, collating packets, etc., I must beat some imaginary internal clock and score keeper.

Most of all, Ego-Pamela must be accepted and loved. Unless others think she is wonderful and tells her so, she is deflated. She feels less than complete. Why do we need others to tell us that we are superior? Why do we need praise to know we have done a good job? Obviously, our sad little souls have yet to realize we are beloved, holy, and whole. Perhaps as children or adults, we were criticized and believe we are inferior.

This reminds me of the beautiful, touching song by Libby Roderick: *How could anyone?* We are beautiful, divine, and loved. The ego just does not know it or believe it.

Not realizing this would bring forth her demise, Ego-Pamela is also obsessed with becoming enlightened. She needs others to believe she has achieved a higher state of consciousness. From the *Blueprint* I learned that Ego struggles to appear and achieve more, suffering with perceived inadequacies. The drama it creates supersedes Essence until we finally realize we are spiritual beings created in the image of an all-knowing, all-powerful, infinitely loving God. Only then can we release false beliefs and behaviors that diminish us. Only then can we let go of addictions that feed the ego so we can express who we truly are.

When we finally acknowledge and embrace the broken parts of ourselves, we can know our perfection and wholeness. We realize we are enough and quit striving, seeking, and searching. With this awareness, we are free to be all that we are. We dance as Essence with all her radiance and glory.

AFFIRMATION:

I am beloved, holy, and whole, free of all attachments so I can embrace and express my Divinity.

DAY 29

From Suffering to Forgiveness

Nobody cares if you can't dance well. Just get up and dance. Great dancers are great because of their passion.
– Martha Graham

CONFESSION:

I have difficulty forgiving others for wrongdoing, especially those who commit horrific deeds to the innocent.

We have been told to forgive and forget, to love our enemies. How is this possible? How can we let those who have committed atrocities off the hook? Why should felons who have killed thousands, taken food from the mouth of babes, abused children, and raped women be forgiven for their unspeakable crimes?

A friend shared that she harbored resentment from the cruelty received from a relative for years. She held onto grievances far longer than necessary. In fact, every time she repeated her sad tale of persecution, she experienced the pain and anguish once again. It was like picking a scab and reopening the wound repeatedly, so it never healed. After years of suffering, she eventually looked within and admitted she participated in the ongoing conflict. Once she took responsibility, the relationship healed.

I recall being at the bedside of my husband's aunt as she lay dying of metastatic breast cancer. Even in her last days, she berated two of her sisters for mistreating her. For the previous twenty-five years, they had maintained a feud about a silly clock. No one could even remember how it started or why it occurred. As I stood at the bedside, I was compelled to speak. "Auntie, you are dying. It is time to forgive and make amends. Instead of taking this resentment to your grave, wrap your negative thoughts in a pink bubble and let them float out the window. Then maybe you can find some peace before you take your last breath."

I could not believe what came out of my mouth. It was as if someone took over my voice and said these words. My mother-in-law, sister-in-law and stepdaughter who were at the bedside, were equally appalled. Their jaws dropped and they stared wide-eyed at my seeming insensitivity. However, the next morning our dying aunt asked to see her sisters. They hugged and forgave each other, and she died peacefully a couple of days later. What a blessing for this moment of forgiveness. What a shame they wasted all those years maintaining a grudge and harboring ill will.

During my father's final days, I received a quasi-apology for something he did when I was a teenager. We were going on a family outing and because I was ready early, dad told me to wash the car. I did not want to do it because I wore a white dress, and I didn't want to get dirty. He told me I did not have a choice, so I washed the dirt off with a soapy sponge and he rinsed the suds with a garden hose behind me. My older sister came outside and asked why I was washing the car. I said that Dad made me do it and under my breath said that I hated him. Dad heard me and put the garden hose in my face getting my hair and dress-soaking wet. Then my sister said, "I'm sure she really loves you now." When he asked, I said I did, fearing he would do something worse if I told him how I really felt. Then my sister said I had obviously lied because how could anybody love someone who treated him or her like that.

I cannot remember what happened afterward, but the emotional scar remained as one of the most diminishing and painful experiences of my teenage years. My sisters were also deeply affected by this incident. One of them reminded Dad about it a month before he died and told him he needed to ask for my forgiveness. Instead of saying "I'm sorry," Dad said he was told he owed me an apology. Since he could not even remember the incident, this was the best he could do and all I could expect.

I forgave him years ago, but I never forgot. In fact, the pain surfaced again when I read an article in the paper about a mother was charged with abuse. She went to jail for thirty days for turning a hose on her son. She claimed she could not get him to go to bed at a decent hour and resorted to using water to get him to comply since she could not spank him.

In the Scriptures, we have been told to forgive seventy times seven. That is 490 times! I understand why we need to forgive repeatedly because our memory keeps painful experiences alive. Familiar scenes and incidents bring painful memories to the surface, and we feel them again. But what about those who continue to hurt others? Do they deserve to be forgiven if they keep making the same mistakes repeatedly?

Forgiveness is possible only if we see beyond outward appearances into the very soul of the individual who is responsible. There we recognize Essence, the truth of being, which can never hurt anyone. Since we are one, hurting another means we also hurt ourselves. Only a false persona that takes over when we fail to express our Divinity is capable of crimes and atrocities. Only Ego, the part of us that is angry, jealous, deceitful, manipulative, and unaware could do something so bad. Unless someone is mentally ill, on drugs or disconnected from Essence, they could not hurt another human being and feel no remorse. And only Ego refuses to forgive.

I used to believe that everyone must pay for his or her crimes, the old "eye for an eye" law of the land. If we forgave someone, we were letting them off the hook and they would not have to pay for their misdeeds. Like many others, I failed to read the rest of that sacred passage in Matthew 5:38-39. *You have heard that it was said, 'Eye for eye, and tooth for tooth. But I say unto you, Love your enemies, bless them that curse you, do good to them that hate you, and pray for them which despitefully use you, and persecute you.*

Through the *Blueprint*, I now know forgiveness is an inside job. When we forgive others, we free ourselves from the bondage of negative feelings and resentment. We are the ones who suffer by holding grudges, not the person who we hold accountable for our suffering. Lack of forgiveness keeps us in victimhood.

In his book, *Radical Forgiveness*, Colin Tipping shares a transforming approach to reconciling pain caused by another. Instead of remaining victims and blaming them for what happened, he encourages us to shift our perception and embrace everything as being for our highest good. When we transform victimhood with gratitude, we become whole. With this quantum leap in awareness, we can go one-step further. We realize forgiveness is no longer even necessary. No one is right or wrong. We accept what is and know that we will be stronger and more aware for having the experience. In fact, Tipping believes we "contract" with others before birth so we can raise our vibration. Knowing this, we truly can do nothing but bless our enemies and turn them into friends.

Forgiveness also demands we view ourselves in a different light. When we realize we are no longer helpless victims but co-creators of our lives, we must accept some responsibility for what happens. At the same time, we cannot blame or pass judgment on ourselves. Certainly, we do not deserve to be hurt. Only when we can see the blessing in the pain will we be able to let go and choose peace. Instead of being right and holding a grudge, we can heal. Instead of suffering, we are free.

While this is true, we still need to ask for forgiveness for wrongdoing. If we hurt others by our words, thoughts, and deeds, even when we know they are Ego's doing, we need to apologize. Asking for forgiveness is not easy, but we do it because it clears the debris from our psyche. We will wallow in pain from our past mistakes until we make amends. This is what my forty-day cleanse is about. By confessing, I am purging my soul of residual negativity and suffering. Only then will I be free to fully embrace and express my Divinity.

Affirmation:

I embrace all experiences and encounters as blessings, knowing they are critical for my soul growth. There is nothing to forgive.

Day 30

From Calloused to Compassionate

Stars are always dancing. Sometimes they dance twinkling away with the rhythm of your joyful heart and sometimes they dance without movement to embrace your heartache as if frozen sculptures of open-armed sadness.
– Munia Khan

Confession:

I am quick to respond and often say things without realizing others can be hurt or offended by my remarks.

I believe I am a compassionate person and can communicate effectively. I have read many books and attended workshops on these subjects and even taught volunteers how to actively listen. However, I still have a long way to go in the communication department. Just ask my husband. He gets annoyed because I interrupt him and complete his sentences, impatient for him to get the words out. Impatience is just the first of many shortcomings that interfere with relationships.

Communication becomes even more challenging when someone is hearing impaired or lacks understanding on the topic. A classic example is a long-distance phone call I had with Mother about a new printer/copier my sisters and I gave to her for her birthday. Instead of letting someone set it up, she purchased cartridges for her old printer to print greeting cards for the next four months. I was angry that she wasted money on unnecessary ink, and I was irritated that someone had not yet installed her new printer. Then I learned a couple family members offered to assist and Mother refused. In my annoyed state, I am sure my comments were accusatory, direct, and loud since she is hard of hearing. She claimed I "yelled" at her, and our conversation ended on a negative note.

Not willing to let this go, I called back an hour later, apologized, and tried to be more constructive. I discovered she did not realize her new printer was also a copier. After explaining the features of her new equipment a few times, she understood. Then I ask how many cards she needed to print before I visited in two weeks and installed her new printer. Again, it took at least four repetitions to discover that she only needed three cards and she already had some in her files. I suggested she use what she had on hand and encouraged her to leave the cartridges for the old printer in the packaging, keep her receipt, and return them. Obviously, I had jumped to the wrong conclusion and assumed Mother was resisting change. I truly need to get my facts straight before reacting!

Years ago, talking with my ex was even more difficult, especially in the car. When he drove, I offered helpful hints. If he did not respond, I did not know if he could not hear because he was deaf in his right ear, if he had another route in mind and was dismissing my suggestions, or if he was ignoring me because I had insulted him. Poor communication was only one of many issues in our relationship.

This experience encouraged me to become a more diplomatic side-seat driver. Since I cannot stop myself from being helpful, I take a breath and use humor to keep things light. Below are some examples of how I more tactfully interject pointers on the road.

- Your significant other is speeding, it is a holiday weekend, and the police are out in full force. You think, "You are an idiot. Would you just slow down before you get a ticket?" You pause and say, "I sure hope the police are on their coffee break."

- The light turns green, and you are sitting for what seems like minutes instead of seconds. You think, "Any time today would be nice." You take a slow, deep breath and say with a smile, "This must be your lucky day. That was a very short red light."

- You are fast approaching your exit and your partner is speeding along in the passing lane. You think, "Where the hell are you going?" You smile and say, "I can't believe we are at our exit already." Hint! Hint!

Communicating is easier if we follow the advice of Don Miguel Ruiz. In his book *The Four Agreements*, we are encouraged to "Be impeccable with your word. Speak with integrity. Say only what you mean. Avoid using the word to speak against yourself or to gossip about others. Use the power of your word in the direction of truth and love."

As this sage advice sinks in for a minute, I realize I have a long way to go to be more effective in conversing with others. Am I gossiping in my journal or dissing others and myself through these confessions? I certainly want to be more compassionate, caring, and constructive in my relationships and my communications. Instead of being in a hurry, I will think before speaking. I typically just react. What pops into my head immediately escapes uncensored out of my mouth.

A friend told me about an incredibly wise and enlightened woman who responds to every situation with a neutral "Oh." Whether she is informed of a crisis or a blessing, her response is the same. She accepts what is and lives above the drama of life. She does not interject her opinions or judgments but allows what is. This reveals yet another flaw of mine. I believe I know what is right or wrong and do not hesitate to express my opinions, whether anyone wants to hear them or not.

Years ago, I wrote a poem/prayer entitled "Soften My Spirit." I should hang it on my office wall as a reminder. The first stanza reads, "Soften my mouth so I no longer speak sharp words that cut the hearts of others. Let me communicate with kindness and understanding so everything I say is reassuring and uplifting." Maybe if I read this every morning and follow my own advice, I will be able to communicate more effectively and compassionately.

Marshall Rosenberg describes an effective process in his book, *Nonviolent Communication – A Language of Life*. Step one is observation—describe the concrete actions we observe that are affecting our well-being. Step two is feeling—express how we feel about what we observe. Step three focuses on our needs—describe our needs, values and desires that are related to these feelings. Step four is making a request—ask for a concrete action that we need to enrich our lives. By sharing what we see, feel, need, and want, we avoid blaming others and making assumptions.

No doubt, we all could use some lessons to converse more effectively. We can all become more conscious of how we express our thoughts, feelings, and concerns. By taking a breath before we respond, we can be more sensitive in expressing ourselves and in relating with others. I am determined to listen more attentively and think before I speak, to focus more on understanding others rather than expecting them to understand and agree with me.

Affirmation:

I communicate with kindness and consideration; I listen effectively and judiciously share my thoughts, feelings, and opinions.

DAY 31

From Pretense to Transparency

Dancing is creating a sculpture that is visible only for a moment.
– Erol Ozan

CONFESSION:

I am eager to share my stories, ideas, feelings, and knowledge, revealing more than most probably care to know.

It is obvious to family and friends that I love to talk. I do not hesitate to tell all to a friend during our half-hour walk each morning. I divulge the latest saga in my family's extreme drama and feel better for sharing. I appreciate the opportunity to be brutally honest with a caring listener and gladly return the favor. We have an even exchange.

This forty-day confession process is also about radical truthfulness and transparency. As I peel off the layers of protection and performance that are integral parts of Ego Pamela, I purge my soul. Once I have stripped down below the false persona that I present to the world, the naked truth of who I am is being revealed. Spiritual masters agree that authenticity is critical for our awakening. So how much do I really need to expose? Isn't anything sacred? Can't I keep some of my sordid past private, yet still be free of guilt and shame?

My husband and I saw the movie T*hanks for Sharing*, about participants in a 12-step program for sex addiction. Since I have never been a Friend of Bill's or attended a meeting, I was curious about the process. What amazed me the most is the support given by sponsors. Their 24/7 availability is crucial for guiding both newbies and medallion-carrying members beyond temptations. The movie showed how years of sobriety can be poured down the drain when times get tough. Triggers are everywhere, and each challenge can knock even the most dedicated off the sobriety wagon.

On my spiritual journey, I have fallen from grace many times. I have been stuck in the rut of victimization and have followed false prophets down footpaths to nowhere. Fortunately, I am blessed with spiritual mothers who encourage me to face facts. These kindred spirits are committed to my soul growth and do not let me get away with anything. We share all and hold each other accountable. We also protect each other's privacy. What is shared during our time together is for our ears only.

For four years, I participated in a Mastermind group that met weekly. We followed their standard process and began our sessions with affirmations about surrender, a greater power, readiness to change, forgiveness, intention, gratitude, and service. Then each took a turn sharing our latest issues and concerns, dreams, and desires. These dedicated souls insisted I not play victim but take responsibility for my role in conflicts and their resolution. We were committed to shifting perceptions and seeing the blessing in painful experiences. By refusing to perpetuate old beliefs and negative patterns, we learned together to live in truth.

Spiritual friends do not agree with us. Nor do they always confirm our perception that we are correct, and the other person is wrong. They also do not support our justifications for reacting or retaliating. Instead, they call us to a more conscious way of being. We receive guidance and encouragement to take the higher pathway and be all that we are. No feeling sorry for ourselves; no wallowing; no excuses.

DAY 31

In *A Few Good Men,* Jack Nicholson made his famous declaration, "You can't handle the truth." Being transparent and facing facts may be tough, but with dedicated soul sisters and brothers on our side, it is possible to face facts.

While the Mastermind process is like the 12-step program, it goes further. At some point in our healing journey, we are transformed. When we perpetuate our addiction story instead of affirming, "I am beloved, holy, and whole," we feed the part of us that is broken. Only when we let go of our negative past will a quantum shift occur so we can embrace and express Essence. I view this as the thirteenth step.

Healing occurs at depth and can even alter our DNA. The genes that manifest as addiction can be transmuted. After all, we are just masses of dynamic energy. A shift in consciousness will eventually create changes in the physical body. As the Law of Mind Action states, "A thought held in mind will produce after its own kind." Therefore, we fake it until we make it. We dress like a diva, sing and dance like a diva, until we feel like a diva, and eventually, we are a diva. We change ourselves from the outside inward until we realize the truth of our being.

Truth and transparency are important in the transformation process. To be honest, I must admit that I love telling my spiritual story. I like being centerstage. Many people think I am an excellent, engaging speaker and my messages are uplifting. Since people learn through parables, perhaps it is good to share.

When I offer guidance to others, it reinforces what I have learned and helps me to continue to grow. I also enjoy facilitating healings for others because in the process, I, too, am healed. We are one, and when one benefits, we all do.

I have searched my soul to make sure my efforts are not Ego in disguise. When I do a healing, I am in the state of openness and receptivity. Loving energy flows through me, and I become the hands and heart of God. I just show up, a willing participant in the transformation process. The same is true when I speak or do a workshop. I am present, turn myself over to a higher power, and become the voice of God. What comes forth is perfect. This is the reason why I am committed to sharing the *Blueprint*. It is not Ego-Pamela, but Essence that expresses. Amazing! I have my answer!

I will continue to bare my soul and strip away the façade until only Essence shines through in all her glory. I will do my best every day to convey the truth of my being and look through eyes of love to see only the Divinity in others. This is who/what we are.

We discover even more about our sacred nature and are free to realize our highest potential when we remove Ego's mask. By sharing our story, we touch the hearts of others and encourage them to do the same. As we come together and cleanse our souls, we raise our vibration and uplift all humanity. Nothing could be more perfect; nothing could be more helpful and necessary in these chaotic times.

Affirmation:

I am an open book and embrace transparency, encouraging others to cleanse their souls and discover their Divine Essence.

Day 32

From Greed to Generosity

You have to love dancing to stick to it. It gives you nothing back…but that single fleeting moment when you feel alive.
– Merce Cunningham

Confession:

I am not generous with my money, but I often give too much of my time and energy for activities that are not my priority.

A friend recently confided that a loved one is generous to a fault. She gives gift cards to everyone who helps her and pays more than invoice price if she thinks she was not charged enough. Unfortunately, her funds are limited, and she often goes without necessities. She also has great difficulty accepting gifts and feels obligated to return the favor. Since her financial circumstances have changed, her family encourages her to alter her behavior to no avail. The pattern continues and her children pick up the slack, dreading the moment when they will have to intervene and assume responsibility for her finances.

Another acquaintance rests on the opposite side of the generosity continuum. She lives in a state of lack and is stingy with her funds, time, and energy. She learned to use the system to acquire as many benefits as possible and stashes money away for rainy days that she is convinced will come sooner than later. She also does not hesitate to ask for help, but never reciprocates.

I have not been very generous with my funds since I have not earned an income for many years. However, I did have a tendency to give too much of my time, talent, and energy to worthy causes. I was a full-time professional volunteer. This meant I may not have anything left to dedicate to the *Blueprint*, my priority and purpose. I stepped back from many commitments to other organizations last winter while I was ill but am still tempted to jump up and say "Yes!" when I am honored with a request to serve. The latest opportunity was for a position on the Board of an organization that is close to my heart. While this was tempting, I turned down the offer so I could remain true to this writing project and other *Blueprint* endeavors.

A couple of years ago I helped our church launch a capital campaign to build a new sanctuary. It was a huge success. The pledges exceeded our goal and are coming in ahead of schedule. The consultant for the project was astounded at the results. According to all his charts and data, we should only have been able to bring in a third of the required amount. Our positive approach and spiritual energy are far different from what the consultant ever experienced before. Most churches crack the whip with a "give until it hurts so you will have more jewels in your crown" strategy. We had a positive philosophy of "radical generosity" where contributions were viewed as an opportunity to shift consciousness.

Giving should not hurt or leave us wanting. When done out of habit, pride, or to get something in return, energy shifts into a negative mode. Unless we give freely, with an open heart and without any thought of the results of our efforts, our actions come from Ego, not Essence. Conscious giving promotes the flow of loving energy and opens wide the door to abundance. When we share our bounty with purity of spirit, we give in a manner which is in harmony with our resources. Instead of excessive giving out of compulsion, our gift is inspired and uplifting.

Giving launches the "Circle of Abundance," another revelation from the *Blueprint*. Generosity creates a vacuum, a space for us to receive blessings in return. What comes back to us will not be the same thing that we gave, but it will always be greater than we gave, and it will be in perfect Divine Order. The movie, "Pay It Forward" perfectly illustrates how the Universe works. Positives multiply exponentially. We should not wait for someone to do something nice for us but should start the process.

Receiving completes the cycle of abundance and is just as important as giving. Without the ability to graciously receive and gratefully accept what is offered, giving is tainted. The flow of goodness is impeded, and we can spiral down into a state of scarcity.

A few years ago, Mother received a new robe for her birthday. She had worn her old one for so many years, the collar was frayed. Instead of immediately wearing the new one and disposing of the old, she put her gift in the dresser and let it "age" for a year or so. We could never decide if she did not like the new one and was being polite, if she was trying to win Ripley's oldest and rattiest robe award, if she was a master at delaying gratification, or if she did not think she deserved new things. Regardless of the reasons, her response generated negative feelings and great frustration among those who purchased gifts.

When not balanced with receptivity, giving becomes the epitome of selfishness. In fact, when goods are provided and remuneration is declined, benefits are minimized. In the workplace I discovered that the more you charge for services, the more valuable they seem. Free seminars are perceived as being useless or ineffective and are not well attended.

This reminds me of my former tendency to offer healings without charging a fee. When someone scheduled an appointment and inquired about payment, I informed them that I accepted love offerings. Now my actions and beliefs come into question. Didn't I feel worthy enough to receive compensation? Weren't my services valuable enough to merit payment? Didn't my clients benefit enough to reimburse me for my time, efforts, and energy? On one hand, my ability to perform intuitive healings is a gift from the Universe and, since it is free to me, I have the freedom to pay it forward and bless others. Perhaps a far deeper issue is involved. Since I did not receive payment for work that I performed as a child, maybe I believe that I do not deserve compensation. Food for thought!

In 2006, *The Secret* was published and became a best seller. It showed how we can manifest good and abundance in our lives and encouraged people to be proactive. However, many used this strategy only to acquire material things. Do we really need more stuff? I believe we need more love, peace, and joy in our lives and in the world. Instead of manifesting or sharing goods, we can share intangibles. A smile can brighten someone's day; a hug can transform sadness; a compliment can make someone feel special; a call can remind a lonely person they are close in heart and prayers. These expressions of love mean far more, require so little, and cost nothing.

Generosity of spirit can also transform a relationship. Despite how others treat us, we can be kind and compassionate. Instead of reacting negatively to snubs and snide remarks, we can see past the pain that is expressed and embrace the divinity yet to be revealed in the other person. We can avoid years of suffering and conflict by sharing our infinite supply of love. Since every thought, word, and deed has the potential to heal, we can transform the world one blessing at a time.

AFFIRMATION:

I bless others by generously and joyfully giving my time, talent, and treasures, and through my positive thoughts, words, and kindnesses.

Day 33

From Separation to Oneness

On many an occasion when I am dancing, I have felt touched by something sacred. In these moments, I felt my spirit soar and become one with everything that exists.
– Michael Jackson

Confession:

I am attached to my story, my drama, and would like to truly know oneness with all.

Although I feel connected with others and the entire Universe, I have yet to experience a deep level of Oneness explained by a few enlightened souls. I watched a YouTube video of Dr. Rick Linchitz speaking at a "No You and No Me" conference. He shared how a health crisis stripped him of all that had been important in his life and opened the door to Oneness. Although he told his story, he said that it was the past and did not feel like himself anymore.

I recall the moment I first felt connected with everything. In meditation, I envisioned that I was standing and looking out over a beautiful landscape. As I reached out my arms, I could feel powerful loving energy flowing between me and everything around me. Even today, as I recall this experience, tears come to my eyes at the intensity of the emotion I felt. Maybe it was just deep compassion, but the connection felt very real.

I realize that until I truly know Oneness, Ego-Pamela will continue to dominate. She needs to feel singled out and special. Until Essence and Ego are united, I will continue to look at people, circumstances, and occurrences with eyes of judgment. I will see things as right and wrong. Instead of observing with impartiality, I will continue to believe I know what is best and what is appropriate.

In the world where people suffer and experience pain, how can we be indifferent to their plight? How can I be in this world but not of it? A shift in perception will no doubt make all the difference. I truly wish to see clearly.

On Sunday, the minister spoke about how our beliefs about ourselves have evolved. We used to think we were physical beings having a spiritual experience—a body with soul. Then we believed we were spiritual beings having a physical experience—a spirit with body. Now we know we are spiritual beings enjoying a spiritual experience in a spiritual world. Everything is Spirit.

Quantum physics confirms this to be true. Everything is energy and empty space. It just appears solid. Even very dense objects like rocks have slow-moving electrical fields. Because of our senses, we perceive things as being well defined. We see and feel where we end and where they begin. We sense that we are separate physically from every object in the world. When we step back out of the latest drama, we observe from a different perspective. We see the entire Universe as a whole and ourselves as part of this huge organism.

Perhaps this is the key. We need to step off the stage of life and let go of our many roles to get out of the latest scene. With this change in our point of view, we are no longer an actor in the drama of life. In fact, some days I would like to be far away from the latest crisis in my family, but do not know how. As an empath, someone who deeply feels what others experience, I am not sure I can separate myself from what is going on around me.

A couple of days ago, my sister received a three-quarter inch splinter in her finger as she was installing a wood floor in her living room. She passed out when she tried to remove it herself and had to get another sister to help.

I felt her pain and was immediately concerned that she would not be able to work in her hair salon if her finger become infected or she had nerve damage. As quickly as these negative thoughts flowed into my mind, I let them go. Fortunately, her finger is fine, and she worked through the following day without difficulty. Even from a distance, I was caught up in the drama. Is it possible to be compassionate without becoming embroiled in someone else's story?

Separation also occurs when we live in the past instead of being fully engaged in the present. When attached to the past, to the pain and suffering that is part of our history, we are unable to live in the moment. Each time we share our story, we relive the past. We go through the trauma one more time. However, this is how we learn. The Bible and most sacred texts are filled with parables and stories about how others overcame challenges and temptations. Their universal language of myth and symbols touch us at a deep level. We do not need explanations to grasp the moral of the story. It has been passed down to us in our genes as part of the collective consciousness that is sensed by all.

Although Oneness is at the heart of its teachings, the *Blueprint's* matrix structure consists of many distinct cells. Each one has an archetype that I experienced in meditation. Through their stories, I was able to integrate critical teachings into my life and make core shifts in consciousness. Now the well-defined structure of the *Blueprint*'s matrix is morphing into something formless. The well-defined spheres of existence—quantum, self, social, global, eternal—have morphed into fields that are more fluid. The dimensions of life—physical, mental, emotional, intuitional, spiritual—have blended into a holistic unit.

I no longer need to look at life experiences one separate aspect at a time. I also sense another dimension is emerging, a state of being that is beyond the all-knowing, all-powerful, infinitely loving, ever present eternal realm. When I am ready, I am sure it will appear. And I believe it will have everything to do with Oneness.

A spiritual mother, the one who sent the YouTube link mentioned previously, is a student of Oneness. She shared how letting go of drama and our story was an important step in the process. I know intellectually that we are One and feel a very deep connection with our amazing earthly home and all its inhabitants. I also know that separation continues to wreak havoc in the world. Every day the news reports how belief systems lead to terrorism, genocide, abuse, entitlement, and other atrocities. We choose political sides and bash opposing candidates and positions. In addition, we feel justified because we believe we are right, and the other side is wrong.

This separation explains the myth of Adam and Eve. When they ate of the fruit of the tree of knowledge of good and evil, they became separate from each other and all Creation. They were banned from the Garden of Eden and were symbolically separated from Source. Only Ego believes it is disconnected and detached. Essence, our spiritual nature, is One with God and All That Is. Until we embrace the truth of our being, we can avoid thinking separate thoughts and speaking separating words: I, me, my, self, we, our, they, them, etc. Maybe if it looks like One, acts like One, and talks like One, it eventually will know and be One!

AFFIRMATION:

I release my story and the past to embrace this sacred moment and know Oneness with All That Is.

DAY 34

From Scarcity to Sustainability

There was still not likelihood that we could make a living from dance. We were doing it because we loved it.
– Alvin Ailey

CONFESSION:

I have tried to please others and spread myself too thin instead of focusing on one or two activities that could sustain me.

I recently spent an afternoon with two soul sisters. After a healthy lunch, we shared our goals, dreams, and current projects, then provided feedback and ideas. One theme that pervaded our discussion was "sustainability." In other words, what activities and projects will not only feed our souls but also put food on the table?

To be honest, I have not made decisions based on potential income since I married my second husband. I have had the luxury of allowing him to provide for me and have not worried about paying bills. Maybe this has been a copout and now it is time for me to choose activities that are more financially productive. I already made one major shift when I resigned from all volunteer projects and positions. This freed me to focus on my own work. By pursuing efforts that are both valuable and viable, I will be able to do even more.

Sometimes it feels necessary to compromise values and deepest desires to generate cash. Funds get low, and good jobs are scarce. We think our only option is to grab what we can to survive. If we truly believe in an abundant Universe, and if we really are connected with Source, we do not need to settle for second or third best. Obviously, life is not this simple. Common sense must prevail. We still have one foot on planet earth and one in the realm of the Divine. While living a spiritual life as a spiritual being, we still have bills to pay and meals to prepare.

I may not have had to choose between what I love, versus income-producing activities, but I have had to put work aside to care for my husband, stepdaughters, and ailing parents. These challenges tested my strength, endurance, and resolve. While I wanted to escape to an isolated cabin surrounded by tall evergreens on a mountaintop, I did what was necessary. And I did it willingly. After fulfilling my duties to the best of my ability, I went back to what I love most—sharing the *Blueprint.* Now I believe I can focus on what will both uplift humanity and sustain me. My efforts will be meaningful, in alignment with my higher purpose, and they will generate a salary.

In the *Blueprint,* the concept of win-win-win emerged. I was aware of win-win solutions, but a third win was new to me. I discovered that conscious choices produce results that are not only good for us and the other party, but they will also sustain our earthly home. When we make enlightened decisions, we all thrive, and Mother Earth will be preserved for future generations. The synergy generated by this three-point Circle of Abundance, is another amazing revelation from the *Blueprint.*

During our time together, my soul sisters and I discussed when and how we are inspired. I shared how I was guided to begin my forty days of journaling confessions. I knew I was ready to get back to work, but I did not know which of my numerous incomplete projects to tackle. I explained how I typed a statement in my iPhone before going to sleep, affirming that I would receive guidance on what activity should be my priority.

Before I received guidance to journal confessions for forty days, I considered focusing on my Higher Tea® project. Divine inspiration had led me to write a book, create an ongoing women's tea circle, and package the concept for other groups. With more marketing and follow up, I could sell a lot more books and launch many more women's circles. Through these efforts I could also acquire more speaking engagements and generate substantial income. My program has the potential to expand throughout the entire Unity Movement, churches, and community groups, blessing millions of women. What is stopping me? No doubt, it is my lack of follow-through, lack of focus or the preference to create new initiatives instead of promoting existing ones. I have many reasons for my lack of success, and it is time to quit making excuses.

One classic defense is the lack of support. This one must now be retired. During our discussion yesterday, my soul sisters and I realized how much we could help each other. We have different skills and experiences that we can share. I have published a book, am an expert in program planning, and have some expertise in marketing, including the ability to make excellent PowerPoint slide presentations. One in our group is a talented musician and knowledgeable about creating e-books and Internet marketing. The third is an artist and videographer with a great deal of experience and expertise in writing. Each of us also has diverse connections with experts and resources that can provide valuable training and guidance for product development, marketing, and program implementation.

We feel extremely blessed to have reconnected and know we will benefit from the synergy of our collective efforts. This is what happens "when two or three are gathered in My name." Together we create synergy and can achieve far more than we can alone. In the marketplace, we might have competed, but as conscious colleagues, we are committed to each other's success. Instead of expecting and needing positive feedback, we are open to suggestions that can move us forward in our efforts to live purposefully. We want to serve the world with our unique form of love, and we are committed to doing it in an efficient, effective manner, one where we will not be depleted physically, financially, or spiritually. To this end, we embrace the concept of sustainability in our unique ventures. We are committed to working smart, not simply hard.

Each of us recognizes the need to narrow our focus and address only one or two ideas at a time. This may be challenging as our creative minds have opened doors to so many possibilities. Unless we prioritize and concentrate on one or two, we will spin our wheels, dilute our efforts, and run out of steam. Unless we divide larger projects into small, manageable, and achievable activities, we will not succeed. We also realize that we may need help from experts in a variety of fields to make our visions become a reality.

My friends and I will continue to support each other and meet regularly every few weeks. What a joy it is to have kindred spirits in your corner! What a blessing to know that conscious choices can ensure our efforts will not only uplift humanity, but they will also sustain us in the process.

AFFIRMATION:

I seek guidance so I can serve in a manner that not only uplifts humanity, but also sustains me physically, fiscally, mentally, emotionally, and spiritually.

Day 35

From Negligence to Accountability

Life is the dancer and you are the dance.
– Eckhart Tolle

Confession:

I am accountable to only myself and fail to follow through on many commitments.

I have never been a fan of Weight Watchers because I did not want anyone to know exactly how fat I was. I did not want to weigh in and air my dietary laundry in front of other slim wannabes. Nor did I want to confess to the fact that I am addicted to sweets and sneaked snacks when no one was watching. Isn't it interesting that I am now so eager to tell everyone I have lost over thirty pounds, given up gluten, and rarely consume sugar or milk products? Yes, I confess; I am a master at minimizing my failures while broadcasting my successes. I am also eager to share my success and encourage others to adopt a healthy lifestyle. How typical of Ego!

One of my primary excuses for not following through on commitments is that I am accountable to only myself—and Spirit, of course. When I held professional positions for the American Cancer Society and Prevent Blindness America, and even as a volunteer member of boards and committees, I answered to others. We developed plans of action, and everyone knew exactly what they were supposed to do by when. We also reported on a regular basis. This is how goals, great and small, are achieved.

When working solo, as I have been doing for over twenty years, I have not had the luxury of partnerships. I may have had a concrete plan with tentative timelines and well-defined objectives, but I could easily stretch them out or put the project aside to accommodate other priorities or new interest. When other parties are involved, we cannot slack off. If we do not fulfill our obligations, we compromise our integrity. By joining forces with those of like mind and intention, like my "Soul Sister Support Circle," we become accountable to others. We express our intentions, map out a strategy, and report in. Of course, we are free to make adjustments, but if we drop the ball, our partners are the first to know. They remind us of our vision for the future and keep us true to our sacred vows.

For the solitary sojourner, support systems are a huge blessing. Not only do our associates offer constructive feedback and link us with beneficial resources, but they also champion our causes and applaud our accomplishments. Because we are one, we are committed to each other's success. We help each other remain true to our higher purpose and ourselves. My current group has come into my life at the perfect moment. How typical of Divine Order! I need all the help I can get to share the *Blueprint* with the world.

One recent endeavor was my one-woman show about my spiritual transformation, *Confessions of a Spiritually Promiscuous Woman* (http://www.veniceunity.org/media-library/video-archive/111-dr-gerali-show/). I had no choice but to follow through after the world premiere was scheduled and marketing plans were launched. I had to put the finishing touches on the script, integrate movements and props, and practice until it was second nature. I had no choice but to be ready to rock on opening night. With support from kindred spirits, this program was implemented eighteen times around the country and was very well-received.

In the future, I intend to transform this journal into a book. This forty-day soul cleanse has been such a powerful experience that I must share it with others. I want everyone to follow this amazing process and know what it feels like to let go of residual baggage and inner garbage.

These are ambitious goals, but I am ready, willing, and able. I feel physically healthy and strong. I am focused and determined to remain true to my vision. They will become a reality, not because Ego Pamela loves to be on stage and in the limelight, but because divine inspiration and guidance will make it possible. I know that these and other sacred ventures will materialize when Essence is allowed to express in all her splendor. As I remain open to the possibilities, they emerge easily and effortlessly.

The Enneagram system of self-discovery includes the personality pattern of the dreamer. These people may have brilliant ideas in their minds and hearts, but they never transform them into reality. Unless they become builders and convert intangible concepts into concrete form, they will never achieve their highest potential. Dreams can come true only if we take one small step at a time toward our goal. By joining with others of like mind and being accountable to them on an ongoing basis, we can more easily realize our heart's desires. The support and encouragement we receive makes all the difference.

I have accomplished a great deal on my own. However, my forward progress has been in fits and starts. Sharing the *Blueprint* has always been my objective, but I have not always been able to follow through on my commitment. Good intentions are never good enough. I have lacked perseverance, singularity of purpose, and discipline to remain true to my Self and my reason for being. Now, with extra support from kindred spirits, I am better able to walk my talk and fulfill my divine contract. No more empty promises!

Journaling is also helping me to remain true to my aspirations. As I confess my shortcomings, they seem to dissipate. By stating my concerns in written form in front of God and the entire world, I am putting myself out there. I have declared to the Universe and to my conscious self what my intentions are. This led to the birth to my newest *Blueprint* babies—my second book and show.

To fulfill my higher purpose—sharing the *Blueprint* with the world—I need to get my act together with a singularity of purpose. I need all the focus and determination that I can muster. To transform inspired ideas into realities, I will also welcome all the input and encouragement I can find. Every available resource must be mobilized. Fortunately, we are part of an abundant Universe, one filled with everything we need to uplift humanity in our own unique way. I have my work cut out for me, but I am excited and energized because the motivation comes from a higher source. And it does not feel like work. This time, instead of giving lip service to a bright idea, I will do it. My soul sisters will keep me on track and true to myself. For their encouragement and for the opportunity to live on purpose, I am profoundly grateful.

AFFIRMATION:

I embrace and prioritize ideas that are divinely inspired and offer them as my unique service to humanity.

DAY 36

From Pride to Humility

I feel that the essence of dance is the expression of man—the landscape of his soul. I hope that every dance I do reveals something of myself or some wonderful thing a human can be.
– Martha Graham

CONFESSION:

I have flaunted my many talents and accomplishments while minimizing my shortcomings.

I am proud of my talents because I worked extremely hard to develop them. Is this wrong? I used to be embarrassed when people complimented me. As a teenager, I was introverted and insecure. I wanted to be inconspicuous. I felt insignificant and unattractive, especially since I was forced to dress like my sisters in clothing that was not stylish.

Once I leaped from my shell, I did not mind being in the limelight. My creativity blossomed, and I worked hard to complete my education—Bachelor of Science in Nursing, Master of Public Health, and Doctorate in Holistic Health Science. I took pride in my efforts, and the more I accomplished the better I felt about myself. I also received more recognition. Recently, I was honored as the Very Important Volunteer at our church for starting the women's program and for coordinating the communications for our successful capital campaign. The minister recently reminded me that when I agreed to take on this critical role, he knew the project would be a success.

Am I proud of my accomplishments? Yes! I work hard and always do my best. Is it wrong to feel good about your work? I do not think so, but on occasion, doing well does not guarantee positive feedback.

In college I took a four-week logic class where the professor presented two problems five days a week for four weeks. I solved every problem but one. Each day he asked those who solved the puzzle to raise their hands. Often, I was the only one with my hand up. While I loved the challenge, everyone else was just putting in time because no grades would be given. Once when no one else raised his or her hand, the professor asked me to draw a diagram on the blackboard to demonstrate how I found the solution to a problem. During my explanation, he made a snide remark about women's intuition and questioned my strategy. I put the chalk down, went back to my seat without finishing the problem and refused to get back up. Instead of being gratified with my proficiency, I was embarrassed and annoyed by his insensitivity. I believe he truly did not like the idea that a young woman was obviously smarter and more dedicated than the rest of the class.

The first time I was humiliated in front of others I was in the first grade. We received penmanship booklets and were instructed to write our first name on the back. Later, we were told to write our second name. I must have thought she said to write our name a second time because instead of writing my last name after my first, I wrote my first name twice. It did not make sense, but I was trying so hard to do everything right. Another boy made the same error and our teacher swatted both of us with a paddle. I was truly ashamed, and I never told a soul, not my parents or my older sister. I could not believe that I was punished and degraded so publicly for a simple mistake. Emotional scars like these remain on the psyche for a long time. Perhaps these experiences serve a purpose; maybe they encourage us to work a little harder and do a little better.

As a child, I remember hearing ministers preaching about how bad it was to be proud. They told us "The first shall be last and the last shall be first." They also said, "The meek will inherit the earth." I never understood these teachings because I was competitive and wanted to win. I thought if you finished first, you would be rewarded. Years later, I realized that it is all about motive. The *Blueprint* taught me that there is great value in doing our best and achieving excellence. In fact, to function at less than peak performance is a waste of time and effort. However, if we strive to excel only to beat others and need to be first to prove we are better than others, Ego is in control. Perhaps this is the reason why many religions encourage us to suppress or eliminate Ego. In the fundamentalist church where I was raised, the negative force that caused us to "sin" was an entity known as the Devil.

Early in my spiritual journey, I was not aware of the role humility plays in our soul growth. I only felt the sting of humiliation from a few very painful memories. I know now that when we are humble, we no longer need to be first, best, or head of the class. Ego takes a back seat so Essence can perfectly express the truth of our being. We no longer need to prove our worth to anyone to be all that we are.

Once while performing a healing, a very earnest spiritual seeker asked how she could eliminate Ego. I was surprised but took a deep breath and paused for guidance. Despite my efforts to be serious and reverent, I started to giggle. Then a deep, dramatic voice said from within, "Oh, you mortals and your Egos! Instead of trying to purge yourself of Ego, use your personality and character traits to live purposefully. Instead of rejecting this part of you, integrate it to be all that you are." How interesting that instead of bashing Ego, we were encouraged to embrace and use it to glorify God.

A few years ago, I had an amazing meditative experience that demonstrated the difference between pride and humility. While listening to classical music I felt myself go into a deep, dark hole. I was trapped in the blackness, and I could not get out no matter how much I struggled. Then I was still. I listened to the guidance and learned all I needed to do to get out of this bleak situation was to make my own wings. This seemed odd, but instead of questioning the wisdom that came from within, I began to fashion a pair of wings. They were exquisitely made of peacock feathers with rows and rows of beautiful iridescent eyes. While creating my wings, I realized that I chose feathers that were symbols of intuitive powers. In fact, fortune tellers and gypsies often wear a peacock feather to let others know they have psychic abilities.

After I completed this mental creative process, I put my wings on and easily rose from the darkness into the light. When I reached the top, I put my wings down and felt truly blessed. Others could not see the magnificence of my wings, but they were there in all their glory for me to use whenever I needed them.

I later learned that the peacock is both a symbol of pride and humility. When its tail is open and when it arrogantly flashes its magnificence, the peacock represents pride. When the tail is down, it represents the opposite—humility. We can choose from these two possibilities. We can strut our stuff with vanity for all to see, or we can simply do our best in the state of unassuming service. When we choose the latter, we humbly give without expecting rewards or recognition.

I now realize what humility is all about. It is not about hiding our talents under a bush or diminishing ourselves with false modesty. We are made in the likeness and image of God and have unlimited potential. As we joyfully and eagerly express Essence, we become our best Self. We become the hands, heart, and voice of God. I vow to do my best and know that everything I accomplished is due to divine guidance and assistance. When my motives are not for Ego gratification or glory, anything is possible.

Affirmation:

I let my light shine by sharing my talents and doing my best to uplift humanity without the need for recognition or rewards.

DAY 37

From a Punishing God to a Higher Power

Do not be frightened, friend. Let us dance our way to God.
– Kamand Kojouri

CONFESSION:

My idea of God has changed so much that I am not sure what I believe or what to call it.

As a child, I was taught to fear God and thought God was a very scary guy. He was a huge, powerful man who knew our every thought, word, and deed, including the number of hairs on our head and how long each one of them was. Therefore, if I cut my hair, God would know, and I would be punished for this sin. The God of my youth was a stern and vengeful judge who terrorized us with threats of eternal punishment for the smallest infractions.

I was also told that I was going to hell just for being born. Since the first couple disobeyed God's edict and ate from the tree of knowledge of good and evil, they were banished from the Garden of Eden by a very unhappy heavenly father. This mistake led to the concept of original sin, and everyone since that moment has been tainted.

I also believed that the Bible came straight from the mouth of God to the ears of holy men in the form of the King James Version. A day of creation was twenty-four hours. Heaven was somewhere up there for the saved, while hell was a lake of fire down there where sinners were tossed. Jesus was physically coming back to earth very soon, and if I did not confess my sins and accept Christ as my Savior, I would go down, not up when I died.

At that time, I did not realize the Bible had been translated many times and included some inaccuracies. In addition, I was not aware of the symbolic nature of its teachings since we were supposed to read every word literally. I had not evolved to the point where I could squeeze truth from its misinterpreted and misconstrued messages. My inner teacher had also not yet revealed herself, so I remained clueless, fearful, and doomed.

Since I was a religious rebel, I pushed these fundamentalist teachings aside when I went to college and focused on my studies. Then, work became my religion. My gods were a substantial paycheck, position, prestige, and power. I did not have time to worry about heaven, but subconsciously hoped my good deeds would open the pearly gates.

In my late 30's I became a student of spirituality and experienced profound changes in my perceptions about God, heaven and hell, Jesus, sin, and the Bible. A positive presence replaced the nasty Grinch of my youth. God was no longer a super-parent who provided for my needs if I was good and punished me harshly when I made mistakes. God became a friend who provided comfort and support if asked. When I discovered meditation and spent more time listening instead of telling God what I wanted, I sensed something far greater. In a state of gratitude, I felt loved and connected with this higher power. In the silence, I received guidance that seemed to emerge from an inner voice. From these experiences, I discovered that God was not just out there, but also in me. However, God still seemed like a separate entity, an omnipresent, omniscient, omnipotent force that conducted the symphony of Life.

To be honest, I do not like using the word "God" because it has been so adulterated. However, it is short, sweet, and easier to say then Higher Power, Divine Mind, Spirit, Presence, Universal Intelligence, Jehovah, Creator, Allah,

Brahman... There certainly are as many names as there are perceptions and pathways to God. God is not a destination. Some do not even think of God as a proper noun.

In his book, *God is a Verb: Kabbalah and the Practice of Mystical Judaism*, Rabbi David Cooper claims we should avoid viewing God as a masculine noun because "It" is not a thing, but what we do as enlightened souls. In addition, it is not about actions, but about being. I love the idea that God does not have a gender, shape, face, or location. God just is All That Is. To be honest, I do not even think of God as being good because this requires judgment. Also, if everything is God and good, how can we explain the negative things that happen in the world?

This leads to another question. What are we, as part of this massive, ever-expanding Universe? I often say, as do many others, that we are beloved children of God, created in the likeness and image of God. If this is true, then what we are depends on our perspective and our understanding of our Higher Power. Since our belief system changes as we become more aware, so does our concept of ourselves.

When God is no longer a judge or punishing parent, we can no longer be victims subject to that which happens "to" us beyond our control. As we become seekers of truth and awareness, we discover that we can make things occur "by" our intention and the power of positive thinking. When God becomes a friend, we learn we are vessels of co-creation, and things materialize "with" our active involvement. Later, as seers and knowers, truth is revealed "through" us as we allow the voice of God to speak.

Only when we finally realize we are spiritual beings and One with God can we look in the mirror and see God expressing. Then we can show up every day "as" the Presence of God on Earth. No wonder the spiritual journey is so confusing! No wonder we constantly strive to know who we are! Every time we discover something new, we must change our thinking to accommodate our evolving perception of God, the world, and ourselves.

In *The Mystic Heart: Discovering a Universal Spirituality in the World's Religions,* Wayne Teasdale describes commonalities in the major religions of the world.

He shows that if we remove man-made rules and dogma, common universal truths are discovered in all mystical teachings. One is the belief in a higher power, a force greater than we are. All religions except Buddhism embrace this concept. Perhaps someday we can embrace our similarities and oneness instead of accentuating our differences. Wars are fought and millions are killed because people with differing religious beliefs have decided that only their idea of God is right. Nonbelievers are labeled as infidels or heretics and become targets for annihilation or evangelism. How could anyone believe a benevolent Higher Power would condone killing? How can anyone use God as a rationale for murder and mayhem?

I have not only struggled with the idea of God, but also Jesus. Since he was the son of a terrifying God, I feared him as well. For years, I could not even say his name aloud. The "J" stuck in my throat like a fishhook. I could also never understand why those who attend the church of my youth end every prayer with "in Jesus' name, Amen." Obviously, they are not aware of the error in translation and the directive to pray in my "manner," not in my "name" or to me.

After years of reinterpreting the teachings of Jesus, I began to see him in an entirely new light. Now he is one of my primary guides—not savior, but teacher and way-shower. After all, he was a radical rabbi, mystic, and healer. Because of my negative upbringing, I nearly tossed the baby Jesus out with the Bible bathwater, baptism, and belief system. In fact, until I became a student of spirituality, I did not understand the distinction between our inner spiritual nature and religion with all its rules and rituals.

The human experience is about becoming more aware or enlightened. We are not going anywhere, and we will not find anything when we get where we think we are headed. We only need to realize and express the truth of our being. Instead of striving to solve the many spiritual riddles, perhaps we just need to allow them all to remain a mystery. It is. God is. I am.

Affirmation:

I release the need to label and understand the nature of God and enjoy every moment I am aware of the Presence of the Divine.

Day 38

From Flawed to Innocent

It doesn't matter if I'm off the beat. It doesn't matter if I'm snapping to the rhythm. It doesn't matter if I look like a complete goon when I dance. It is my dance.
– Dan Pearce

Confession:

I have made many mistakes and am far from innocent or pure in heart.

The story of Adam and Eve in the garden is about lost innocence, which can be seen as an allegory. They ate from the tree of knowledge (became aware) of good and evil (judgment) and were removed (separated) from the Garden of Eden (God/Source/Self/Heaven). With a conscience (awareness), they saw (transparency) their nakedness (sinful nature) and were no longer innocent (pure being). The rest of the Bible focuses on how we can recover our virtue. This is our story, the tale of how we return to a childlike state of innocence by becoming more aware.

We begin as pure, honest, open, loving, joyful, peaceful, playful, curious, creative… children. We are unaware and unadulterated by the knowledge of our differences and do not feel separate from others or God. We see through eyes that are free of judgment. In fact, infants are not even able to distinguish between themselves, their mothers, and the rest of the world. They are

connected with their surroundings. Then they grow up!
The Jewish culture celebrates the thirteenth birthday with bar mitzvahs or bat mitzvahs. It is the moment when boys become men and girls become women. This is the age of accountability, the time when young people are viewed as being capable of making choices on their own and of knowing the difference between right and wrong. Prior to this point, their parents were responsible for keeping them in line. Now they must have the inner discipline to say "No" to the bad and "Yes" to the good. Unfortunately, our brains do not develop frontal lobes and the capacity to make sound judgments until we are twenty-one or older. At thirteen, we are not yet ready to make critical life choices.

A friend taught school in a county jail. She had a thirteen-year-old student who killed his grandparents and showed no remorse. He was diagnosed as a psychopath. Although he had reached the age of accountability and was being tried as an adult, was he accountable? He did not seem able to make good judgments. He was not of sound mind because no one in his right mind could murder those who took him in and cared for him.

My friend had great difficulty working with this boy because he seemed vacant, soulless. He showed no emotion, no passion, no interest in anything or the future. He went through the motions waiting for his trial. I encouraged her to just show up every day as the Presence of God and see beyond the blank stare into the essence of his being. It was still there somewhere, screaming to be recognized and acknowledged. Unfortunately, he hanged himself in his cell before the trial could take place.

As a child, I heard many times the story of how Jesus embraced children as he talked to the masses. When the adults wanted the children removed so he could teach without interruption, Jesus explained something extremely critical about our awakening. I never knew what this story meant or what heaven had to do with being childlike until I relived this experience in a guided meditation. This is what I wrote in my journal:

> *I was guided back in time nearly 2000 years when Jesus the Christ was a teacher. I was a seven-year-old girl and Jesus was like a favorite*

uncle to me. As he hugged us and touched our heads, we felt so adored. He was loving and joyful, not at all bothered by us as we played at His feet. Then He said, "Let the little children come to me for theirs is the kingdom of heaven."

In that moment, I knew exactly what Jesus meant. We are to let go of our beliefs, judgments, limitations, and fears to become like children. As children, we can live fully in the present. Only then can we know the perfect state of pure Essence. Only then will we know what it means to be Divine. Children are innocent, joyful, playful, curious, open, and loving. They are free of judgment, guilt, shame, and fear. In that sacred moment I knew how it feels and what it means to be accepted and adored as a beloved, innocent child of God.

This image and experience were the perfect representation for the Eternal realm of being of the Blueprint. It shows that we are One with God/ Source. All thoughts of separation are eliminated as this perfect child represents pure consciousness. In this state, we can express our Divinity through our Humanity. Reborn as innocent "children," we are Essence, pure love, peace, and joy, that which we truly are.

This archetype of the beloved child of God revealed what it feels like to be innocent. I now know it is possible to return to this state despite the many mistakes we may have made. The slate of our sordid past is washed clean. This is what it means to be reborn—to let go of false beliefs, and to know and embrace that which we are.

Some cultures like the American Indians believe that every time we choose the wrong path, we give away a piece of our soul. Through sacred rituals, holy men help individuals to find and return missing pieces to restore them to a state of wholeness. Maybe this is the reason it is so important to forgive ourselves. We let go of the past so we can experience only the perfection of now. At this moment and every moment in the future, we are whole. We are pure, free from all that we have or have not done. It is a return to innocence.

Perhaps this is the reason why I am engaged in this forty-day confession process. All my mistakes and misperceptions are coming to the surface to be released or transformed. Then I can be free and clear. It is a purification process. I am being cleansed of the past so I can experience every moment in a state of innocent awareness, one without judgment. Confessions are helping me to step outside this body and observe what Pamela is doing and thinking. Instead of seeing my faults and shortcomings, I see only Essence expressing. She is not tainted by the errors of her past but is pure Love and Light.

As I journal this morning, I am filled with emotion. Tears are flowing. I know that I have reached a pivotal point. I have a new realization of what I am. There is a new heaven (Divine Mind/Essence) and a new earth (Self/human expression) that reveals the truth of my being. I look out the window and see the beauty around me. It is exquisite. Each intricate part of Creation functions effortlessly in perfect harmony with all others. I think of the people in my life and imagine I am looking deep into their eyes. I see only beautiful souls. Individually, we are complete and more than enough because we are pure Essence. Together, we are part of the Universe integrated into one perfect, synergistic whole. Nothing is missing. Nothing is less than perfect. All is well and in perfect Divine Order.

It is a new dawn, a new day, a new heaven, and a new earth. I am beloved, holy, and whole, innocence personified.

Affirmation:

I am free of the past and express Essence every moment of every day in a state of innocence.

Day 39

From Animosity to Unconditional Love

To be creative means to be in love with life. You can be creative only if you live life enough that you want to enhance its beauty, you want to bring a little more music to it, a little more poetry to it, a little more dance to it.
– Osho

Confession:

I have struggled to be good enough to deserve love and have mistaken attraction and mutual interests for love.

Although I felt loved as a child, I do not remember my parents saying, "I love you." We were not coddled, pampered, or praised. I also do not remember receiving heart-warming hugs. Mother is so reserved she usually puts her hands on your shoulders to keep you away when you try to get close. Dad always managed to get past her defenses. When he came home or left the house, he made a beeline for Mother, playfully teasing and kissing her despite her objections. However, Dad did not hug or show affection to my sisters and me.

Mother surprised me one day when she described how she felt when she discovered she was pregnant with me—she cried because she loved my older sister so much, she did not know how she would find enough space in her heart or enough love to give to a second child. She must have discovered an infinite supply because she had five children!

I was working as a nursing assistant the summer when I got engaged the first time. While making a patient's bed with an orderly, I told him about our plans and explained that I would be getting married in six weeks before I went back to college. When he asked if I loved my fiancé, I listed all the reasons why getting married made sense. We were both students at the University of Pittsburgh; his G.I. benefits would increase after we got married; we would be able to save on rent if we lived together. My work partner stopped me and said, "But do you love him?" I do not remember what I said or how I felt at the time. I am sure I thought that I was in love, but at nineteen, I had no idea what love was.

Whatever we felt for each other was not enough because the marriage fizzled after a few years. My ex had no time for me and did not seem interested in, or supportive of my activities. As a medical student, he was either on call, studying, or sleeping. During the ten years I was single between marriages I dated a lot of bar slugs. They were all attractive, but lacking in substance—not financially, but in character. Perhaps at the time I was as shallow and superficial as they were and was not ready for a deeper relationship.

Fortunately, the Universe blessed me with an ideal mate the second time around. My husband is a handsome, successful, compassionate, and passionate man who adores me. I have a partner who accepts the changes that are occurring within me on my spiritual quest. He does not mind being the straight man when I give humorous spiritual talks and willingly schleps whatever I need for performances.

Several years ago, we had dinner at a Chinese restaurant. While waiting for the check, I eagerly broke my fortune cookie in two and read the message aloud. It stated something about being involved in a love triangle. Immediately I denied this and said, "This one must be yours because I'm not having an affair. Are you?" My husband in all his wisdom replied, "No it's yours. It is you, me, and God, and I know where I stand." Don't you just love a man who knows his place!

Over the years, I have learned that love is far more than physical attraction and romance. I have deep connections with my soul sisters and spiritual mothers. I also feel an instant link with creative people. Soon after I remarried, and while a newbie on my sacred journey, I was concerned about the instant bond I felt toward other creative spirits, including members of the opposite sex. I discovered that the energetic connection was at a deeper, spiritual level and not romantic attraction.

We cannot genuinely love another unless we love ourselves. Unless we open our hearts and know our wholeness, we are not able to let others close enough to know how Oneness feels. When we finally open, we become vulnerable to potential pain of separation and rejection. This became truly clear as I helped clients heal relationships and mend broken hearts. We symbolically sewed fissures in the heart or closed cracks with crazy glue and laughter. We even used an imaginary laser to heal damaged tissues. The results were all the same. Wounds from the past can only be transformed by Divine Love. The pain melts away and we are free to love again.

I have also learned through healings that relationships, even the most positive and fulfilling ones, are only a taste of what we truly desire and experience when we know Oneness. Those who search for a partner and insist their soul mate is waiting for them often receive guidance that what they truly crave is union with God/Source/Self. Obviously, having a soul mate and a wonderful relationship with a husband/partner is an amazing gift. However, we can become sidetracked in the physical domain on our quest for the real thing.

Some people are hard to love. They do and say things that are unattractive and hurtful. When these individuals are family members, things get complicated. We may love someone because they are blood, but we may not necessarily like or respect them. When we cannot accept their choices or their actions, tough love may be our only option. Boundaries need to be established and painful decisions may be required to protect ourselves from painful encounters.

I learned from the *Blueprint* and life experiences that Divine Love far exceeds physical attraction. When Ego and all its insecurities fade into the background,

Essence expresses as Love. It is so profound that what we sense on the outside no longer exists. We look with eyes of pure Love and see the Divine in the mirror and in others. Only then are our hearts open wide enough for Love to pour forth and fill up the entire Universe.

On our spiritual quest, we also discover that heart trumps head. We learn that the intellect and ability to understand will only take us so far. With an open heart, we no longer need laws. The Ten Commandments become irrelevant because we could never cheat, steal, lie, or hurt another person. We would treat all with kindness and compassion. We would always observe the Sabbath—a day of rest—because we would honor ourselves and provide necessary down time. Every moment would be holy as we always put God first.

We would also never take the Lord's name in vain. Since I AM is the name of God, we would never diminish ourselves by saying I am stupid, I am unworthy, I am weak, etc. When the heart is open, we can fully embrace that which we are—Essence, pure Spirit, and pure Love. And we will see and honor all others as the same. Namaste!

AFFIRMATION:

I am Essence expressing that which it is—pure Love—and generously share it with everyone who crosses my path.

DAY 40

From Suffering to Bliss

I will build you up again, and you, Virgin Israel, will be rebuilt. Again you will take up your timbrels and go out to dance with the joyful.
– Jeremiah 31:4

CONFESSION:

I have never been in a state of true bliss and am jealous of those who have experienced it.

Today is my final confession and I am filled with emotion. The time went by so fast. When you are in the flow, everything comes easily. There is no struggle. No effort is required in the process when Spirit leads, and we allow.

At the same time, memories that bubbled to the surface have not been easy to face. Some have opened old wounds and brought pain and suffering to the surface. Difficult or not, this was necessary to clear the soul. After a period of illness and lethargy when meditation, writing, and studying seemed impossible, I am back on track. I am inspired instead of feeling frustrated and apathetic about my life and work. Through this amazing forty-day process, doubt and criticism disappeared. Everything is possible with God and Ego Pamela has taken a back seat. The work is being done. Ideas and words emerge and with them, the best comes forth. Essence is expressing.

On a few occasions, I have had moments of elation. When I tap into the universal databank and segments of the *Blueprint* are revealed, or when I share its spiritual wisdom and practical guidance, I am beyond excited. During powerful meditations where the skies open and I receive amazing revelations, I experience flashes of ecstasy. When I perform healings, I sense the infinite possibilities of the Eternal realm. These sacred sips of rapture are fleeting, while the extended period of joy I have experienced through this exercise has been continuous.

This spiritual high feels like a mystical mania. My energy level is through the roof. I am inspired, euphoric, and more passionate about this process than I have been about anything in a long while. It must be obvious because many have commented on how bright my eyes are and how intense my energy seems. Although I have committed only to a forty-day journaling process, I do not view this as a temporary venture. I intend to continue rising early, meditating, and journaling every day. Is this continuous moment of joy, which has lasted throughout this entire process, the illusive state of bliss?

Eckhart Tolle spoke about being in a state of bliss as he sat immobile on a park bench. My experience is the opposite of stillness. I am flying. I want to tell everyone about it and how it has affected me. I am impassioned, energized, and ready to embrace the next step. My journal will become a book to share with others. I am compelled to publish what I have learned about transparency and encourage others on their path of transformation.

I recall what Charles Fillmore said about zeal in his book, *Twelve Powers of Man.* At age 94 he said, "I fairly sizzle with zeal and enthusiasm and spring forth with a mighty faith to do those things that ought to be done by me!" Wow! It is time for me to get started, to embrace that which is mine to do—sharing the *Blueprint.* The time is now. No more stalling. No more excuses. No more going in circles and repeating old patterns.

I am also deeply grateful for what I have learned from this intense experience. It has been so powerful that I can hardly contain myself. That is an interesting statement—*I can hardly contain myself.* It is as if I am larger than life, greater than the former, small self. The enthusiasm that courses through my veins extends far beyond the boundaries of my physical body. It seems like the Chaos Theory, which states, "Something as small as the flutter of a butterfly's wing can ultimately cause a typhoon halfway around the world." No doubt, the force I feel can have a powerful impact on humanity. The benefits can spread exponentially to uplift others. As I generously and joyfully share my experience and ideas, I know that they will. The sky is the limit, and I feel like I can fly!

This reminds me of two StoryPeople® prints that hang in my powder room. One reads, "For a long time, she flew only when she thought no one else was watching." The second is, "These are multi-purpose wings and when she's not flying, they accessorize nicely with almost anything." Well, I have wings and, like my dad, I love to fly. He still buzzes me on occasion. I sense his presence every time I see a cardinal. This dancer is tapping her toes and flapping her wings, filled with infinite potential. I am free to soar to heights of awareness I have not reached before. I am free to be the voice, hands, and heart of God in a way that I have never known before.

I also seem weightless, as if I have taken a quantum leap to another dimension. Perhaps this is what a shift in consciousness feels like. I am more alert and sense life more intensely. I am free of negativity from my past and the guilt, shame, and fear that held me back. Not only am I free of limiting beliefs, but I also have clarity of vision and purpose. A familiar song keeps going through my head: "*I am free, I am invincible. There are no chains that bind me. I am free, I am invincible right now…*"

I am also sad that my forty days of confessions are over. At the beginning, I was not certain if I could fulfill my commitment. However, once I started, no effort was required on my part. It happened through me, not by me. It has been so empowering I do not want it to end. I want the motivation and flow of energy to continue. Although the forty days are over, I know this is just the end of the beginning. I cannot wait to see what comes next.

Sometimes I wish I did not have earthly distractions, so I could focus more on my work, but balance is crucial. I need to find a way to stay on course when I am on vacation, or have company, family obligations, or social commitments. I intend to continue my practice of rising early for meditation, and then will pick up my pen. I will remain observant and present, knowing each moment will bring something new, something special to deepen my awareness or solidify my knowing.

Today and every day I will express my Divinity through my humanity in every way possible. I am willing, ready, and able to do as Spirit leads. I am physically strong, deeply passionate, and totally committed to whatever comes next. I could not be happier, and I am free to be all that I am. The tether that bound me to attachments has been severed. Now I can defy gravity as Essence.

I am so grateful for this rebirthing experience. This purification process has freed me to express the truth of my being. However, I am still human and will experience moments of sadness and pain in the future. And I will make mistakes. Life will offer many more opportunities for me to learn and grow. For now, however, I am beyond bliss.

AFFIRMATION:

I am filled with pure joy as I live every blissful moment realizing my highest potential as a loving expression of God.

EPILOGUE

From Arrogance to Grace

Through synergy of intellect, artistry and grace came into existence the blessing of a dancer.
– Shah Asad Rizvi

CONFESSION:

I failed to remain true to my process and fell in a heap from my spiritual high.

Since this transparency experience was to foster extreme honesty and cleanse the soul, I have one more confession to make. I have been on a spiritual high the past few months and almost believed I was invincible. I was inspired and highly productive. Every day I received incredible guidance. Resources materialized effortlessly as I concluded the rewrite of my forty-day journaling experience. I boasted and became arrogant about my spiritual acumen. Just when I thought I had nailed Essence, Ego reared her nasty head and I fell from grace like a blundering boob.

I have many excuses for my irrational behavior, the first of which is family commitments. They took precedence over my sacred routine, and I skipped a couple mornings of quiet time. Without meditation and journaling, I failed to remain in a state of Presence. Because of this, I felt disconnected from Spirit. Old resentments and ineffective patterns floated to the surface, allowing angry, aggressive Anna to appear. I had no idea she dwelt in the recesses of this sweet, spiritual being. I was dazed and devastated that I could act so offensively and spew such venom.

I was so shocked I considered abandoning or postponing my goal to release this book. I thought I had cleansed my soul and was beyond making serious mistakes or plummeting back into Ego's clutches. But NO! Certainly, if I could sink that far below the pinnacle of perfection that I thought I had attained, I had no business presenting myself as a spiritual teacher or healer. I truly felt like a fraud.

I have not yet grasped all the underlying issues that contributed to this outburst and decided not to make excuses. However, when someone says, "the devil made me do it," I know what they mean. Some offensive entity seemed to have invaded my body and created havoc. Surely, I could not be so insensitive and out of control.

The Universe was obviously cognizant of my shortcomings and provided a course correction. I quickly received the opportunity to scrutinize my actions, seek forgiveness, and get back on track. Long after my apology was accepted, I continued to chastise myself. Doubt crept back into my consciousness as I struggled to remove the hook with its multiple, painful barbs.

Eventually, wounds heal, and we release old baggage, but they never completely disappear. They are stored in our memory banks and remain part of our soul's history. Through grace, however, innocence is restored. We are free from the bondage of our mistakes long before we can forgive ourselves.

As I reviewed my journal entry for the final day about bliss, I was astounded at how high I had been flying. No wonder I crashed! The wax on my faux wings melted and I fell to earth in a heap. I have picked myself up and cleansed my soul—again. Now I am reconnected and moving forward, but with greater awareness and humility. I am more cautious, determined not to spiral into egoic idiocy again. Whoever said, "The higher you fly, the farther you fall," was right. I hope that the harder you land—assuming you gain greater awareness from the experience—the higher you will bounce back.

I wish that after completing this transforming experience I will never falter or make mistakes again. It would be nice if we could be so conscious that we were no longer subject to temptation. But alas, we are human and are never beyond bumbling. We are blessed with faults to keep us humble. On occasion, we will commit errors. We will hurt others and ourselves. Ego might even make desperate attempts to block us from realizing our dreams, but Spirit is stronger, and Essence is our true nature. Instead of groveling when Ego tries to knock us off center, we can stand up, dust ourselves off, make amends, forgive ourselves, express gratitude for the lesson, and resume a purposeful existence.

What I can confirm from this most recent refinement is that each time we falter, we learn—the hard way—to be more cognizant and conscious. Every mistake is a blessing because we dig deeper and purge a little more of the residue hiding within. In this case, I needed another lesson to complete this cleansing process. Humility is exactly what I required to remind me of how vulnerable we are as spiritual beings. I also needed to experience how critically important it is to remain true to one's process. While I was never big on rituals, my current morning observance ensures my continued soul growth and stability. It keeps me on the straight and narrow.

This experience also reinforced my choice not to follow a guru. They, too, are human and subject to transgressions. Instead, we need to stay tuned to the guidance that comes from the still small voice within. Instead of blindly following another, we must be vigilant to the urgings of our own inner teacher. Through intention and hard work, we can change our behavior, focus the mind, and release negative emotion to embrace new ideas. Journaling, healings, meditation, and prayer help us correct the error of our ways. However, no amount of effort can cleanse the soul. Only grace can wipe the slate clean, restore innocence, and make it possible for Essence to express as the divine diva that she is.

Grace is the ultimate gift from God. It shifts our perception and energy to a higher vibration, making miracles and quantum leaps in consciousness possible. We are blessed with grace, not because of any exertion on our part or because we deserve it. Grace exemplifies the elegance of the Universe with peace and order in the midst of chaos. When needs are met and favors are delivered to our doorstep in crucial moments, we have received a gift of grace.

I am most grateful that grace can erase lapses in consciousness and return us to a state of greater awareness, realigning our thoughts and actions with truth. Only with grace can we make the leap of faith from Ego to Essence and be the loving expression of the Divine that we are. What a gift!

Affirmation:

I gratefully receive every gift of grace and know it makes transformation possible.

About the Author

Pamela Gerali is a visionary and pioneer in personal transformation. She rebelled against the rigors of a fundamental religion and, with guidance from her "inner guru," discovered the *Blueprint for the Human Spirit*®. This inspired model for self-discovery and paradigm for conscious, compassionate living evolved in harmony with her spiritual growth.

No longer a fearful and timid conformist, Pamela freely pursues the mysterious and does not hesitate to bare her soul. When led to meditate and journal confessions for forty days, she experienced a deep soul-cleanse. The shifts in perception were so profound she decided to air her less-than-spotless spiritual laundry in this book.

Although she takes spirituality and her mystical experiences very seriously, Pamela cannot resist the urge to bring a little levity to the subject. Whether seeking clarity on the morality of toe cleavage, sharing her transforming story through her one-woman show, *Confessions of a Spiritually Promiscuous Woman*, or explaining the *Blueprint* with her extensive collection of hats, Pamela entertains while enlightening her audiences.

Pamela abandoned a rewarding career as a Registered Nurse with a Master's in Public Health to pursue a Doctorate in Holistic Health Science. She now uplifts others with her natural and intuitive healing abilities. She also uses her creativity and exceptional program planning skills to share spiritual wisdom and practical guidance from the *Blueprint*, her passion and purpose.

Pamela lives in Florida in a state of bliss with her husband, who believes his higher purpose is to support her efforts to share the *Blueprint*. She is extremely grateful for this example of perfect Divine Order and for the opportunity to express Essence in her own creative and eccentric ways.

For more information about Pamela, her books, and the *Blueprint*, visit her website: www.DrPamelaGerali.com.

To receive additional gifts from Dr. Gerali, go to:
https://drpamelagerali.com/dee_bonus/

Also by Dr. Pamela Gerali

Higher Tea for the Thirsty Soul. Scheduled for release in 2021

Steeped with more spiritual wisdom and practical guidance from the Blueprint for the Human Spirit. Includes the recipe for joyful living and the circle of consciousness enhanced with tea imagery, symbolism, and ceremonies.

Embracing Authenticity: An Adventure in Self-Discovery. Scheduled for release in 2021

An inner journey into the essence of being that focuses on the personal dimension of the Blueprint for the Human Spirit and the qualities and characteristics of physical, mental, emotional, intuitive, and spiritual aspects of life.

Embrace Your Divine Inner Diva: A 40-Day Exercise to Merge Ego and Essence. 2021

A downloadable guided experience that includes meditation, journaling, and a playful activity. May be used as a companion journal for *The Dance of Ego and Essence: Confessions of a Divine Diva.*

Confessions of a Spiritually Promiscuous Woman. ©2014

A one-woman show about the spiritual journey, this amusing and inspiring show is a multi-media event that includes music, dance, the art of storytelling, PowerPoint, six distinct characters and audience participation. To watch a video of this show, visit http://www.veniceunity.org/media-library/video-archive/111-dr-gerali-show/.

Create CommuniTea with a Higher Tea Circle: A Program Guide. ©2009

Everything you need to start an ongoing women's group, including an introductory video, planning, marketing, and training tools. (Contact Pamela at Pamela@PamelaGerali.com for more information.)

Higher Tea: The Essence of Joy. ©2007

A feast for the soul and senses, steeped with spiritual wisdom from the Blueprint for the Human Spirit; inspires self-discovery and conscious, compassionate living through the simplicity of tea and the recipe for joyful living. (Contact Pamela at Pamela@PamelaGerali.com for more information.)

For more information and to obtain these offerings or view videos, visit: www.DrPamelaGerali.com.

To receive additional gifts from Dr. Gerali, go to:
https://drpamelagerali.com/dee_bonus/

Made in the USA
Columbia, SC
29 June 2022

62485035R00157